Stock Market Cash Flow

*Four Pillars of Investing
for Thriving in Today's Markets*

ANDY TANNER

Stock Market Cash Flow

*Four Pillars of Investing
for Thriving in Today's Markets*

ANDY TANNER

Published by RDA Press

Rich Dad Advisors, B-I Triangle, CASHFLOW Quadrant and other Rich Dad marks are registered trademarks of CASHFLOW Technologies, Inc.

RDA Press LLC
15170 N. Hayden Road
Scottsdale, AZ 85260
480-998-5400
Visit our Web sites: RDAPress.com and RichDadAdvisors.com

Printed in the United States of America
First Edition: October 2013
ISBN: 978-1-937832-06-3

Cover Design by Chris Collins | American Design Co.

122013

Best-Selling Books
In the Rich Dad Advisors Series

by Blair Singer

SalesDogs
You Don't Have to Be an Attack Dog to Explode Your Income

Team Code of Honor
The Secrets of Champions in Business and in Life

by Garrett Sutton, Esq.

Start Your Own Corporation
Why the Rich Own their Own Companies and Everyone Else Works for Them

Writing Winning Business Plans
*How to Prepare a Business Plan that Investors will Want to Read –
and Invest In*

Buying and Selling a Business
How You Can Win in the Business Quadrant

The ABCs of Getting Out of Debt
Turn Bad Debt into Good Debt and Bad Credit into Good Credit

Run Your Own Corporation
*How to Legally Operate and Properly Maintain Your Company
into the Future*

The Loopholes of Real Estate
Secrets of Successful Real Estate Investing

Acknowledgments

None of us can claim sole discovery of everything we have learned in life. Most of what I've learned as a student and share in this book comes from what I've been given from various mentors, teachers, and business partners. It seems that people were placed within my circle at important times so that I could receive vital lessons along the way.

Many people have mentored me personally. Others I have admired from afar. To those who have helped me personally, I wish to say a word of thanks.

Thanks to Brett Eliason and Noah Davidson for their mentorship in paper assets over the years.

Thanks to Robert and Kim Kiyosaki and the Rich Dad Advisors for lessons of context. I feel privileged to serve on the Advisor team.

Thanks to Mike Denison and Alfred Quinn for their contributions to this book. Mike and Alfred help me to say what I want to say when I can't find the words.

Thanks to Mona Gambetta for sharing her talent and expertise in the creation of this book. Making the jump from teaching to writing was a challenge for me. Mona made it possible.

Thanks to Cindy Geddes and Jennifer Costanza for proofing and editing.

Read The Book That Started It All

Robert Kiyosaki has challenged and changed the way tens of millions of people around the world think about money. With perspectives that often contradict conventional wisdom, Robert has earned a reputation for straight talk, irreverence and courage. He is regarded worldwide as a passionate advocate for financial education.

Rich Dad Poor Dad will...

- Explode the myth that you need to earn a high income to become rich
- Challenge the belief that your house is an asset
- Show parents why they can't rely on the school system to teach their kids about money
- Define once and for all an asset and a liability
- Teach you what to teach your kids about money for their future financial success

Rich Dad Poor Dad — The #1 Personal Finance Book of All Time!

Contents

Foreword
by Robert Kiyosaki

Many people believe investing is risky. So they turn their money over to an expert and hope that expert really cares about their money.

That is beyond risky. In today's financial environment, it's suicidal.

Between 1987 and 2006, investing was less risky. Whenever the stock or real estate market got into trouble, Alan Greenspan, the Chairman of the Federal Reserve, would bail out the speculators. It was not long before the public began to believe that investing in stocks and real estate was a guaranteed path to riches.

In October of 2007, the stock market hit an all-time high at over 14,000 and then crashed, bringing down the global economy. Bear Sterns and Lehman Brothers, pillars of the investment community, disappeared. Merrill Lynch, the stock brokerage firm that millions had entrusted their money to, went bankrupt.

In 2008, the new Federal Reserve Board Chairman, Ben Bernanke, began cutting interest rates all the way to zero, hoping to prevent the new Depression. He then began creating money out of thin air.

Who Do You Trust?

It seems incomprehensible to me that people trust their money, their hopes, and their dreams with those who have run the financial industry into the ground. How can they do that? How anyone can trust people who were paid million-dollar bonuses (rather than being fired) is beyond me.

Believing that these *professionals*, many of whom earn far more than you or me, care more about your money than you do, is delusional.

This is why I am thrilled and excited about this book by Andy Tanner. And his timing couldn't be better. If you know that it is time for you to take control of your financial future, this book is for you.

CASHFLOW Games

In 1996, my wife Kim and I launched our financial education board game *CASHFLOW® 101*. **CASHFLOW101** is also known as *"fundamental investing."* Warren Buffett is probably the most well-known of all fundamental investors.

We created the game to help people who know it's time to take care of their own money.

A few years later, we released *CASHFLOW 202*, which is known as *"technical investing."* Technical investing is investing based upon the market trends, the ups and downs of markets. One of the most successful technical investors is George Soros.

Some investors are exclusively fundamental investors. They look at the financial statement of a business, often investing for the long term because they believe in the future of the business. Some investors are exclusively technical investors. They could care less about the strength or weakness of the business. All they care about is the mood, emotions, or sentiment of the market. For example, Apple was the darling of the stock market for years. Then suddenly, market sentiment changed and—although Apple had great fundamentals, great products, and over a billion dollars in cash—the price of Apple shares plunged. Investors who bought stock based upon Apple's strong fundamentals lost.

Smart investors invest based upon both fundamental and technical input. This is why Andy's book is a great book. Andy draws on both fundamental and technical insights before making his investing decisions. I know because I call Andy for his guidance before I invest my money.

And not only is Andy a great investor, he is a great teacher...which means I learn a lot every time I seek Andy's guidance.

What Is Risky?

Millions continue to blindly turn their money over to "experts" they do not know to manage it for them. They seem to have the "buy, hold, and pray" investing strategy. I wish them luck, especially in this volatile and unpredictable world. To me, turning your money over to total strangers is very, very risky.

Andy states, "Risk is the lack of control." This book gives investors like you and me more control in a market that often seems out of control.

If it's time for you to reduce your risk by taking more control of your money, the wisdom in this book is priceless.

The Best News

There is an old saying that goes, "The bull goes up by the stairs and the bear goes out the window."

That means, bull markets are slowing going up and bear markets come down like a rock.

This is good news for people who are both fundamental and technical investors because they know how to make money regardless of whether markets are going up or down.

The best news of all is this: If you are prepared, educated, and experienced, the next time the market crashes—and most investors *are* praying the bull goes back up the stairs—you may be making your fastest fortune ever, as the bear leaps out of the window yet again.

Simply said, as you read this book, you are holding your financial future in your hands.

Good luck,
Robert Kiyosaki

Introduction

It was many years ago that I first picked up the book *Rich Dad Poor Dad* by Robert Kiyosaki. In that book, I found the teacher and coach I'd been looking for.

Now, I don't come from Wall Street. It's a nice enough place to visit, but I don't want to live there. I sure don't want to work there. I'm like Robert; I don't want to work as an employee.

I don't come from college, either. I'm a broken-down basketball player who got a scholarship not because I was some kind of elite athlete but because I could foul. But I knew enough to learn from my coach. And what I learned was how to study the fundamentals from someone who knew more than I did, practice in the real world, and keep my skills sharp by putting them into play. But most importantly, I learned how to win. I took a few classes too—though not enough to get a degree. I left just a few credit hours shy of my degree. I never did learn much sitting in a classroom.

After college, I discovered there wasn't a lot of room in the workforce or the NBA for an ex-college athlete with bad knees and an attitude about punching a time clock.

Thank goodness.

Like most people, I was taught my whole life that I needed to go to school and get good grades so I could get a high-paying job. If I'd been good at that—at going to school, showing up every day just because it was expected, taking tests, repeating whatever the teachers had to say whether or not it made sense—maybe I would've gotten straight As and found that high-paying job. But I wasn't, and I didn't.

Growing up, I struggled with my seeming inability to toe the line and do what was expected. But now, as the economy has collapsed and those "good" jobs have dried up, as all those people who were trained to do what someone else told them are waiting around for someone new to come along to tell them what to do next, I find myself grateful for my struggles.

From the very beginning, I found I didn't value what I was told I should value. I didn't value just getting good grades. I wanted to understand the subjects that interested me. I didn't value being in class if I saw an opportunity to do something more interesting. I didn't value a degree in a subject that was assigned to me by a counselor who saw me as no more than a dumb jock.

Later, after I was out of school and happily married with a great little family to support, I didn't value financial advisers who wanted to charge me for stock tips and one-size-fits-all advice. I didn't value money plans designed to make me dependent on someone else's knowledge.

I didn't understand then that there was any other way to make it in the world. I didn't have a rich dad. I didn't have a mentor to show me the way. It was reading Robert's books that made me realize there was a whole movement in the financial industry of other people who shared my values. And you know what? They were getting rich off those values. I'd found my team.

Starting out it seemed unlikely for me to speak knowledgeably on any topic, let alone paper assets, but today I'm Robert's paper asset Advisor, and I've embarked on a path to never stop learning—and never stop teaching. I don't want anyone else to feel that frustration of knowing that the way the world tries to teach us isn't right but not knowing any alternative.

Mastering the Fundamentals

I got my basketball scholarship because I could foul, sure. I'm a big guy, and even now, even in a pickup game on a Saturday, guys feel it when I set a pick. But I guarantee you I never would've survived playing in college without knowing the fundamentals. My coach never tolerated lazy players. We all ran drills, we all showed up for practice, we all ran full-court, with sore knees or swollen ankles, during overtime or extra points, through bad calls or lucky breaks, on home court or away, whether we were stars or players no one recognized. We all knew every play, every drill, every strength and weakness of every opponent. When it came to hoops, we were all serious students.

I'm a serious student when it comes to money. I will never stop learning. I will always be passionate; I will always be engaged; I will always be active. I will never be an expert. In fact, now that I'm a serious student, I don't want to be an expert. An expert is supposed to know everything. As soon as I think I know everything, I will stop learning. I never want to stop learning now. I have finally realized what a real education is all about.

My hope is that this book becomes part of your ongoing education. It's written with the assumption that you are familiar with books such as *Rich Dad Poor Dad* and *Rich Dad's CASHFLOW Quadrant*. Like all books in the Rich Dad Advisor series, it is written to help you increase your financial education. This is the Rich Dad Mission: to elevate the financial well being of humanity. I hope it inspires you to become or continue to be a serious student, the same way Robert's books have inspired me.

Fundamentals

I'm all about the fundamentals. While I like understanding the high-end topics and can happily spend days studying the most esoteric concept, going down the rabbit-hole of economic theory, history, geopolitics, and socioeconomic analysis, I always start by breaking everything down into the fundamentals. My college counselor would've told you it was the jock in me. (He didn't think I was very bright and liked to talk to me in a way that always let me know it). My wife says I'm a natural-born teacher, and I've got 15 years of teaching successful workshops to give her that impression. My sons say it's because I speak cartoon and can make anything sound funny. Whatever the reason, I like to reduce difficult subjects to their simplest building blocks.

I'll be doing that in this book too. I will introduce you to my 4 Pillars of Investing. The 4 Pillars are the basic building blocks to all investing. Once you've mastered them, you will find everything you do is based on one of these four vital areas of study. Let me make it simple for you. It's how I learned. And if I could learn it...well, just ask that college counselor.

As we go along through the book, we'll build on each pillar. You'll go from learning the difference between capital gains and cash flow to understanding financial statements, reading stock charts, and even shorting stock. It will all make sense by the end of the book. And it will all seem easy as you are learning it.

Walking the Walk and Talking the Talk

I like making things simple. I'm going to explain the concepts that you should learn first. And I will try to make these concepts simple so you truly understand them and how they apply to your investments. Keep an eye out for Build on It graphics that summarize core concepts throughout the book. Watch as the number of concepts in the graphic grows to mirror the way your understanding will build your financial education.

BUILD ON IT

BUILD ON IT graphics summarize core concepts throughout the book.

Along the way you will also expand your financial vocabulary so that you learn to speak the language of the stock market. Don't be afraid of the language. Embrace it. This is your money you are dealing with, so it's critical for you to learn this language. To make it easy, I will translate and simplify new terms and concepts and give you a valuable foundation to build upon. But get used to speaking the language of money and enjoy your newfound fluency. That language will be your entry into other avenues of learning, allowing you to search out more information on your own and continue on with your financial education at your own pace.

I also find it effective to learn by doing. Don't just passively read this book and let the concepts wash over you. Be willing to get your hands a little dirty. I don't mean jumping into the stock market without knowing what you're doing. That'd be getting your hands bloody, not dirty. But be willing to try paper trading.

We all know how foolish it sounds for a new investor to risk all their money on the very first trade. Recovering from a colossal mistake can be really hard. But little mistakes can actually be useful because you can learn a great deal from them. That's why I recommend that beginning stock investors start with paper trading. It's a process of practicing your trades in a real account based on actual stock market activity, but you are using paper money instead of real money.

While paper trading, you will make mistakes. And that's perfectly okay. There is not an investor in the world with a 100 percent success rate. Again, the idea is to learn from the mistakes to continually improve your skills, knowledge, and wisdom. Learn to manage risks, have some fun, experiment—but do it all with paper, not cash.

One of things that gets lost in traditional schooling is the concept that making mistakes is one of the more natural ways we learn. Making mistakes should be okay, but it's not. When I was in college, I was scared of making a mistake. If I failed a test and my grade went down to a C for the semester, I lost my scholarship, I got kicked off the basketball team, I had to leave school. The stakes were high. It didn't matter if making those mistakes helped me learn; all that mattered were my grades.

If you take away the penalties the school system gives us when we make mistakes, then there's no reason for mistakes to bother us at all. Think of it like a child learning to walk. When little kids stumble and fall on their backsides they smile and stand up again for another try. It doesn't faze them in the least. Somewhere along the way we lose that very natural willingness to keep trying. I want you to regain it. Experience is a proven way to master something new. It may not be the fanciest way to do it; it may not be pretty. But I've spent enough time getting up off my backside and taking huge leaps forward to know that it works.

For more practice at real-world financial scenarios without real-world consequences, play CASHFLOW® 101 and 202, the board games Robert designed for the simulation of real investing with play money. These will help you practice your analysis and decision-making skills—and have fun while doing so.

Don't be a passive learner. Start being an active participant in your education now!

Chapter One

Become a Great Investor by Becoming a Great Student

When you hear the words "student," "learning," or "school" you might think about a period in your life that had something to do with words like "classrooms" and "homework" and "lectures." But most of us can also think of times when we had some profound discovery experience outside a traditional classroom environment. For me, there's nothing more exciting than when some piece of knowledge clicks and I get to watch it work. Like the first time I made a layup.

Man, I practiced and practiced my layup. I spent hours, focusing on each of the mechanics—dribbling toward the basket, aiming the ball at that sweetspot, holding the ball right for the shot, making sure I had the correct foot forward at the correct time—and when the ball finally bounced off the backboard and fell through the net? That was a great feeling. Now I don't even have to think about it. A layup comes as naturally as running.

Investing has been the same way—though not nearly as tough on my knees.

If you like the feeling of excitement and possibility that comes with new discoveries, you can look forward to this journey of investment understanding. This book—and how I go about teaching—is different from those stiff Wall Street gurus or talking heads you see on TV. How so? Simple: Their run-of-the-mill advice directs you where *they* want you to go instead of where *you* want to go. I'm on your team to take you only where you want to end up. Because I'm not going to teach you *where* to go. I'm going to teach you *how* to go wherever you want.

We Are Both Students in This Together

I want you to know that I'm a student, like you. I'm hungry for knowledge that is useful. I love the time I spend with my mentors and teachers, and I know that there will always be more to learn. When people claim they have all the answers, I think they lose credibility from the start. Because the topic of stock market investing is so large and ever-changing, no one can know everything about it. It's a moving target, at best.

This book is written to help folks who are beginners or people who see themselves as students with room to grow. Chances are that you and I are on the same path. I might be further along, but we're both in the same jungle.

When I started learning about the stock market, I was sick of being a blind follower. I was dependent on the advice of others, and I didn't have a way to determine if that advice was good or bad. I wanted to make some intelligent decisions and contribute to discussions with my financial advisors instead of just doing what I was told. I wanted to feel confident. You've probably felt the same way with your own financial responsibilities.

We are living in a very tricky time right now. The decisions you are forced to make about your future can be scary if you don't know enough about investing.

This book will help you face the future with confidence. It will give you the confidence to know there are always opportunities for you to profit in any type of market: up, down, or sideways. You won't be dependent upon others or even the direction of the market. With education comes options, and with options comes confidence.

Globally, we are rapidly approaching some very trying times. However, I'm convinced that you can prepare and profit no matter what happens.

Advice Is Not Education

Wall Street experts love to tell us what they think is best for our money, but they never seem to want to teach us anything. They like the relationship uneven. The less you understand about the stock market, the more dependent on them you will feel. They want you to be at their mercy. But I see people who are starving for real knowledge.

The so-called "experts" love to give you lots of advice and opinions. But advice is very different from education. Advice is being told what to do, whereas education is receiving real understanding—the kind of understanding that allows you to make your own decisions as to what to do. Education is transformation.

Today, you have the chance to choose the path of education and all of its rewards.

Transformation Is Evidence of True Education

For me, serving as a Rich Dad Advisor is a much different experience than many people might think. Frankly, my experience has been far more about my own learning and personal development than that of being a teacher. I have the gift of spending a lot of time with Robert and Kim Kiyosaki, and the other Advisors, so my opportunity to learn is both precious and humbling.

Robert, of course, is a very skilled teacher, yet he is also an insatiable student. His passion for education runs deep and is a fundamental part of who he is. He often reminds me of what education is and where the word comes from.

e·duce /Id(y)oōs/

Verb: Bring out or develop (something latent or potential).

Notice the word *potential* in that definition. To reflect upon all that we can choose to become is an exercise that is both exciting and staggering. You and I have the potential to land a 747. We can learn to play a musical instrument. We can learn to prepare a gourmet dish. We have the potential to build a house or sail a boat or speak a foreign language. The list is endless. In this light, the idea of education is elevated beyond the idea of merely transferring information from teacher to student. True education is about a transformational process that changes potential into real power.

Education is the process of empowering us to be able to do something we could not do before. Transformation is at the heart of the Rich Dad Mission:

To elevate the financial well being of humanity

Context and Content

Put simply, context is the big picture, content is the details. Information can be understood in various lights depending on the context in which it is held.

The more you learn about investing, the more convinced you will be of the importance of context. What I mean by that is that many people want to be taught what to do before they are taught how to think. This is backward.

Our context is often revealed by the questions we ask. The kinds of questions we Rich Dad Advisors often hear are along the lines of:

"If you had $10,000, what would you invest in?"

or

"What was the most recent stock you purchased?"

Yet almost no one ever asks these questions:

"Andy, what are you studying right now?"

or

"What is the last investing class that Robert signed up for?"

The first two questions show a context (or mindset) where the key to successful investing is nothing more than parking money in the right place. The wiser person sees investing in the context of being a student and learning and getting better at investing as a whole.

Robert Kiyosaki is a master of teaching context. For example, the CASHFLOW Quadrant does not teach how to buy real estate or how to invest in stocks. Yet it's a very powerful teaching tool because it helps people shift their context. It helps people examine their philosophy and how they approach earning money, whether it's as Employees (E), Self-employed professionals (S), Business Owners (B), or Investors (I).

Part of the power of the CASHFLOW Quadrant is that it invites each of us to examine who we are today and who we would like to become tomorrow. In many instances it suggests a profound transformation. Shifting *context* means improving perspective (the big picture). Studying *content* suggests expanding what we know (or the details) and the how-to instructions.

Of course this book contains content, which will help you learn more about the nitty-gritty of paper assets. But every bit of instruction must be applied within the proper context.

The Education Hierarchy™

It is said that beauty is in the eye of the beholder. I'd say that the same is true with value. The value of some information might be priceless to some and worthless to others. Some education is important to everyone—reading, for example. I don't think there are many of us who can achieve success in life without knowing how to read. But the importance of most education is more subjective than we normally think. What is vital to know and what isn't really depends on your circumstances and your goals. For example, had I actually wanted to become an exercise physiologist like my college counselor had directed, knowing the difference between a tendon and a ligament would be really a big deal. But in my current life as student of investing? Not so much.

It bothers me that those on school boards have the power to impose their opinions on the rest of us. The school curriculum is based on what they think is valuable, and those assumptions can be inaccurate for your life's goals. Some education really matters to the school board but doesn't affect your financial life. Dissecting a frog comes to mind. The school board thought it was vital I learn to dissect a frog in high school. Well, I'll tell you, I'm living proof you can live a good life without being an expert at dissecting a frog. I've done ok. I have a great family. I've made a good life. And the frogs of the world are just going to have to go on their merry way undissected.

Now, if I were going to be a biologist, it might be a different story. It might become vital I know how to dissect a frog. But that's because of my circumstances and my goals, not some universal dictate of a bureaucracy. If I wanted to be a biologist I would be vitally interested in frog innards. I would *want* to know how the insides of a frog work. It would be a driving passion. I would be burning to cut open any unsuspecting frogs I could find. I'd be reading all about frog biology, watching frogs be dissected by experienced practitioners, practicing on fake frogs—anything I could do to learn. Just as it has been for me with stocks.

Perhaps some of the most vital education you can receive doesn't even register on the school board radar screens, but is critical to your financial life. You might never have had a class on living a life without a job, but it may be one of your goals. You have likely never even had a class on the basics of the stock market, but the stock market is what millions of people are depending on for retirement. Evidently, these are trivial matters to the average school board. But these are subjects of vital interest to you and me.

Is that a problem? No. You don't need to wait for someone else to dictate what is vital to your education. Not anymore. Not when you become a serious student, because being a serious student is being an active student. Your financial success is too important to leave it to someone else and their opinion of what's important. I stopped being passive when it comes to education a long time ago.

I submit that becoming a successful investor begins by becoming a serious student. This is my invitation to you. It is an invitation to develop your own education hierarchy. You and I are now free from the school board's assembly-line approach. You do not need to be force-fed from their "like it or not" menu anymore. Value is in the eye of the beholder, and you get to decide what knowledge is valuable to you!

Once you decide what is valuable to you, all of your education opportunities can be categorized as trivial, interesting, important, or vital. Don't waste your time on the trivial. Then be mindful of wasting too much time on that which is merely interesting. Choose to focus on the important and the vital—that's where you can best spend your time, your effort, and your money. When you set your goals, think about what you are learning in the context of the Education Hierarchy™. When you do, you'll find that what you study will be more meaningful, more valuable, and more fun.

The Education Hierarchy™

Vital

Important

Interesting

Trivial

Make a list of classes you took in school and think about where these classes fit into your education hierarchy and reflect on how much or how little you use that knowledge each day. Then make a list of what you think you will need to learn to achieve the goals you have today. As you progress through this book, you might discover that mastering The 4 Pillars will be more valuable to you than anything you have ever studied before.

Traditional schools tend to focus on what they often refer to as "general education." The first two years of a typical college experience usually include learning a few things about a bunch of subjects instead of learning a lot about a few subjects. That's why you'll often see people with majors as diverse as art history and pre-med taking the same classes their freshman year. That has never made sense to me. We might end up well-rounded, but we also end up bored—and we pay for the privilege with our time and our money. And you know what? I don't want to be well rounded. I want to be really, really, *really* good at building cash flow. If I need to dissect a frog, I'll hire a biologist.

That's why the books in the Rich Dad Advisor series are so useful to anyone who wants to learn about investing. And with teaching tied to the four pillars, I promise not to waste your time with things that are merely interesting. Moreover, I can promise you that as an investor you will use each of these four pillars on a regular basis, and you will come to view them as vital in your investing.

BUILD ON IT

Determine for yourself what is vital to your education.

FOUNDATION

The Education Continuum™

The CASHFLOW Quadrant helps us figure out who we are and who we would like to become in terms of how we choose to earn money. The Education Continuum™ helps us to evaluate our current education level and set vital goals related to where we want to arrive educationally and the degree of our transformation. Remember that true education is transformation. It changes us.

The Education Continuum™

Ignorance → Awareness → Competency → Proficiency

As you read this book, you will move along the continuum. Your context will shift as you evaluate where you are on The Education Continuum™ and with each new topic of your financial education.

Ignorance

Ignorance simply means we're not aware of something. If you're ignorant of something, it doesn't mean you're stupid. I've observed that most of the people I teach in my workshops have a college education, and, quite frankly, most of them probably have higher IQs than I do.

My grades in school were pretty average—and sometimes even below average. The only reason I am the one who's often teaching others is that I have been a student of investing for a longer period of time than most people. My mentors have been students of investing longer than I have been. I was smart enough to seek out those mentors—and listen to them.

What you lack in smarts or talent, you can make up for with passion and hard work. Effort is the great equalizer.

Most people don't have a clue about the stock market because it's not a topic that is taught effectively in traditional school environments. Realize that you're a very smart person; you just have not yet focused your full intellect on learning about investing.

What makes paper assets somewhat dangerous is that, unlike real estate and business, almost anyone can buy stock at any time. And many people do. There is very little barrier to entry when it comes to the stock market.

Think for a moment about your country's retirement system. In my home country, the United States, the dominant program is a contribution retirement program called a 401(k). In this 401(k) program, workers take a portion of every paycheck and let the "experts" in the financial industry spend it on mutual funds. The majority of these workers know next to nothing about the stock market: the risks, the fees, the laws, or even the basic details of a given plan. Like a herd of sheep, they are funneled into the stock market by the Wall Street sheep herders.

It takes only a little common sense to break from the herd and say, "I probably shouldn't invest my money in something I don't understand." But evidently there aren't enough "common" people in the herd because the herd is getting fleeced on a daily basis.

When we lose money in an investment, it's most often because of something we don't understand. I know that when I look back at my gains and losses, my biggest losses have come when I was delving into something I did not yet understand. More money is lost due to ignorance than anything else.

Luckily, we can escape ignorance.

Awareness

Moving from ignorance to awareness is a good feeling. It is illumination, it is discovery, and it's awesome. But it's impossible to set good solid education goals unless we discover a little bit about the things we need to learn.

I remember years and years ago when I took my first investing course. The instructor put several stock charts up on the screen and began to teach us about "technical indicators." I remember thinking to myself, "This is one of the most impressive things I've ever seen." I became very excited about what I was discovering. I could see that this was something I was going to want to study and learn more about.

When we have moments of discovery we simply learn about what's possible. It was much the same as the first time I ever attended a concert as a child. The concert featured an extremely accomplished pianist, and I discovered what the possibilities were with that particular instrument. With playing the piano it's pretty easy to feel the distance that exists between being *aware* of what the instrument's potential is and becoming an accomplished musician.

As you read each chapter in the book you will become more aware of what professional investors actually do when they make investment choices. Chances are you will then want to delve even deeper. It's natural to want to move from mere awareness to a more complete level of understanding. That understanding is called *competency*.

Competency

Think of an airline pilot who has passed a written test on flight regulations, but has not yet had a chance to practice what he has learned in the air. Think of a musician who has spent many months in a classroom learning to read music, but has yet to pick up an instrument and practice. Competency is that level of understanding that does not yet translate into ability.

Competency denotes a minimum amount of knowledge and skill to perform an act. In a court of law, a witness would be expected to be competent to testify. But competency is often associated with minimums. In most countries there are minimum competency tests for various professional licenses to practice medicine or law.

Competence denotes the ability to get an A on a written test. But understanding how something is done is not the same as being able to do it. The real world demands proficiency. Classrooms are havens of competency. Classrooms reward competency. You can move through your whole academic life with nothing more than competency.

There is little room for mere competency in the real world. The real world rewards proficiency. It's much easier to *describe* than to go out and *do*.

In basketball, it's easy to draw a play on a chalkboard. It's the easiest thing in the world: just a bunch of Xs and Os, a few arrows here and there. Go out in front of 13,000 people and a couple of blind referees and pull it off—that's a *whole* different ball game. That's proficiency. Step onto even a college-level court and try to compete with just competency, and watch yourself learn the real meaning of getting *schooled*.

Proficiency

Closely related to the word competency is proficiency. Proficiency is a higher degree of competency, and that difference in degree can mean the difference between making money and being wealthy. If competency is knowing the play book, proficiency is education of the play. Competency is the intellectual ascent to the truth. Proficiency is execution.

In my experience, proficiency is a pursuit and not a destination. We can always become more proficient. I hope that you will be more proficient in the stock market next year than you are today, and even more so the year after that. But, as I said earlier, the stock market is a moving target, and as it changes, so will you. As the markets change, as economies change, so will your need for changes in your knowledge base. You can never be satisfied with competence.

People wonder at what moment they will know that they are able to successfully trade stocks and options. I don't know the answer to that question because proficiency is a process, not an event. I compare it to the drum lessons I took when I was a kid. I could always hit drums, but it sure didn't sound very good at first—at least not to my parents. Today I can play in my rock band—and we're not half bad. But it was a long process over many years of practice. There is never a singular moment where you

you say "yesterday I could not play but today I can." There are milestones, however. If you have never owned shares of stock, there will be a day when you begin trading on paper or in a virtual account. There will come a day when you invest a small amount of real money. Then the day will come when you short a stock...and so on.

Over time, you travel along the Education Continuum to proficiency. But you can't always put your finger on when those transitions happen. There are thousands and thousands of drummers more proficient than I'll ever be (and that is true for investors as well), but there are probably many more thousands who are less proficient. I can play in my rock band and enjoy making music without effort. Because of my learning and practice, it's now automatic, and it sounds like actual drumming to most people.

Confusing Awareness with Proficiency Will Cost You Money

Part of the value of the Education Continuum is the humility that comes with knowing that if you are an investor, you are also a student. One of the dangers of the stock market is its accessibility. Unlike playing the drums, you can play the market and not realize you don't know what you are doing. I see some people make the leap to awareness and confuse that with proficiency. Sometimes this happens because of arrogance, and sometimes it's merely from the excitement of discovery. If you keep yourself in check with the Education Continuum, you can avoid the costly tuition of the school of hard knocks.

Powerful Suggestions for Becoming a Great Student

Are you ready to take control of your education and become a serious student? Of course you are. You're the one who knows what you want and what captures your interest. You know what is vital to your education and what is trivial. So let's get down to some studying.

As Robert often teaches, there is a drastic difference between "reading" and "studying." I'm going to help you supplement your reading with activities that will make this a study of investing that will actually apply to all the asset classes—not just the stock markets of the world. If you like the idea of becoming a serious student, the suggestions that make up the remainder of this chapter will ensure you a more rapid and powerful transformation than reading alone.

1. Discuss what you read and share it with others who share your interest.
2. Set education goals, not just lifestyle goals or money goals.
3. Begin working with mentors.
4. Do it now!

When you reach the end of this chapter, start writing down additional ideas of your own. Remember, you are now an active participant in your learning. Bring your own experience, your own stories, your own examples to your learning. And be ready to participate.

Share Your Discoveries with Others

You don't have to become an expert to share what you discover. Let yourself get excited about what you're learning. Share that excitement and your newfound knowledge with someone else.

I have found that teaching is a great way to learn. As you read, keep a pen or pencil handy to mark the sections that really resonate with you or that you feel you need to review. Write down notes in a journal or notebook, adding your own thoughts or examples. Sharing those notes and sections with someone else will help you remember what you learn. Explaining concepts to someone else will help you keep things simple and putting the ideas into your own terms and your own examples and stories will cement them in your brain. You will find that you can remember the things that you read and then share much better than the things you just read and keep to yourself.

Check out the *Cone of Learning* developed by Edgar Dale. Years ago he discovered that reading alone was actually one of the least effective ways to learn something new.

After 2 weeks we tend to remember		Nature of Involvement
	Cone of Learning	
	Doing the Real Thing	
90% of what we say and do	**Simulating the Real Experience**	**Active**
	Doing a Dramatic Presentation	
70% of what we say	**Giving a Talk**	
	Participating in a Discussion	
	Seeing it Done on Location	
	Watching a Demonstration	
50% of what we hear and see	**Looking at an Exhibit Watching a Demonstration**	**Passive**
	Watching a Movie	
30% of what we see	**Looking at Pictures**	
20% of what we hear	**Hearing Words (Lecture)**	
10% of what we read	**Reading**	

Source: Cone of Learning adapted from Dale, (1969)

Consider forming a group with two or three friends who are reading this book at the same time you are, and then meet for breakfast once a week to discuss what you're learning. Be sure to steer clear of forming too many opinions too quickly. Just focus on what lessons are being taught, being sure to build on each section as you learn.

Review Your Education Goals Now

At the beginning of any journey, it is a good idea to set some goals. It's not uncommon to have *lifestyle goals*. And it is not uncommon to have *money goals*. But few people I meet continue to set significant *education goals* once they leave school.

As you complete each chapter of this book, remember to keep setting education goals.

Lifestyle Goals

I'm sure that you and I will always have the desire to improve our lifestyles. We all have that in common. You can think of some of these specific desires for improvement as *lifestyle goals*. As I travel the world and speak at various events I often ask my students to list a few of their goals. Here are some common responses:

- I want to quit my job.
- I want to own a house on the beach.
- I want to own an exotic car.
- I want to travel the world.
- I want to be financially free.
- I want to help and serve others.

Go ahead and make a list of your own goals. Not the goals someone somewhere told you *should* have. But the goals that would make *you* happy. Write them down. No one has to see them; you don't have to justify them to anyone. You know why they are important, and that's enough. Write them down as the first step toward recognizing that you are in control of this journey. You decide what is trivial and what is vital—that is true for every aspect of your life, from your education to your goals.

Dreaming Is Free

I'm alarmed at how little time people spend dreaming these days. Nearly everywhere I visit, times have become so tough that people are concentrating on mere survival rather than making plans for abundance. The conversations people are having now about their finances are too often focused simply on getting by, rather than on achieving their full potential or exploiting their opportunities to the very maximum.

I like to remind people that dreaming is free. It's an indulgence we need not feel guilty about. Wherever you live, you stand on the shoulders of those who went before you. I'm sure you can think of sacrifices made by others that have provided you with opportunities you can seize on this very day. When you think about it like that, not only is it okay to dream, but it's actually a very important activity for you to do. You owe it to those who have gone before you to honor their sacrifices. You *can* enjoy time spent dreaming of the great things your future can hold.

Let your dreams fuel your determination and fill you with energy. Dreams unleash the power of both your conscious and subconscious mind. Dreaming feels good. Dreaming *is* good.

Take these dreams and turn them into goals by writing them down.

Money Goals

We can also have *money goals*. Money goals are different from lifestyle goals. But money goals alone tend to lose their power. They're too vague, too dry.

- I want $1,000,000.
- I want $10,000 a month.
- I want to be free of debt.

For some people, perhaps these statements are more *wishes* than *goals*. But money goals become instantly more meaningful when they grow out of your lifestyle goals.

Let's take an example of a goal to make $10,000. Standing alone, $10,000 is just money.

But if we start with a lifestyle goal, such as to buy yourself a top-of-the-line Harley-Davidson motorcycle, suddenly your heart beats faster and that dream starts to come alive. You might visit a dealership and pick the one you've always wanted. You could sit on it, touch it, and feel it. This becomes a very powerful experience for you.

Now it's time to look at the price tag. How much money will you need to make that dream come true? If the price tag is $11,799, you now have a meaningful money goal. At this point you can choose to buy it outright or set a goal to increase your cash flow to cover a payment of $389 per month. Now your money goal is even more specific.

Education Goals

So how are you going to increase your cash flow by $389 each month? The good news is that earning that extra $389 per month is simply a matter of education and action. Some folks may think the only way to gain that amount is to cut an equal amount from their monthly spending. I don't know about you, but I'm not really interested in giving up anything in my life. But there is another way—a better way. Instead of cutting your current spending, you can decide to learn how to acquire income-producing assets that will create that extra money for you.

What Is Wealth Building?

In a nutshell, wealth building is simply learning how to buy assets intelligently. These assets can come in multiple forms:

- Business
- Real Estate
- Paper assets like stocks
- Commodities like gold or oil

When I look at wealthy people like Warren Buffett, Donald Trump, and Robert Kiyosaki, I see people who have become wealthy because they have become educated about how to buy assets. I imagine they wake up in the morning and ask, "Where will I find an asset I can buy today?" They don't need a hot tip. More importantly, they don't sit around waiting and hoping for a hot tip to find them. They know how to look for and look *at* an opportunity and use their financial knowledge to decide whether to play or pass.

If someone with a financial education wants to buy a Harley, they don't skip their morning latte and put their pennies in a savings account and until they have enough money. They don't put it on a credit card and cross their fingers each month when the bill comes due. They don't get a second job. What can you do when you want to make a lifestyle goal a reality?

- Start a business to earn the $389 per month...if we have a business education.

- Acquire a rental property to earn $389 per month...if we have a real estate education.

- Sell some covered call options to earn $389 per month...if we have an options education.

Now can you see that earning extra income is simply a matter of gaining the right financial education?

As we learn about these different asset classes, we can choose which ones we want to dive into and learn more about. Then we can set specific money goals tied to acquiring assets that will meet our lifestyle goals. We use education goals to achieve money goals to meet lifestyle goals. It's a formula that works time and again for the wealthiest people in the world. And it can work for you, too.

Education gives you power.

BUILD ON IT

**Use education goals
to achieve money goals
to meet lifestyle goals.**

FOUNDATION

When you think about it, you might find it striking that once people leave college, they often look only to lifestyle goals or money goals. Many folks draw a blank when asked about their *education goals* because they never learned to be an active participant in their learning.

The Best Path to Proficiency Is Mentorship

If you're reading this book it's likely that you've also read *Rich Dad Poor Dad*, which is the cornerstone of your financial education. You might take note of the fact that the book *Rich Dad Poor Dad* is primarily a story of mentorship. A great question to ask yourself after reading the book is: "Would Robert Kiyosaki have become successful without the help of his rich dad?" Knowing Robert as I do, I would say absolutely yes. But I would also say that he would have found another mentor. Even after his rich dad passed away, Robert still sought out new teachers and mentors, just as he does today.

When I read *Rich Dad Poor Dad* for the first time, I realized I wanted to find many rich dads to help me along my journey. I am always looking for fellow journeymen who are further along the path than I am. It's just common sense.

If you have ever seen the movie *The Karate Kid*, you've seen a great portrayal of how a mentor can change a student's context for the better. We all know the story, I think. (Or maybe I'm dating myself.) It's the story of a student-mentor relationship that develops when an average kid decides to defend himself against the neighborhood bullies. The mentor agrees to train him, but the boy becomes frustrated almost immediately with his teacher's unorthodox methods. Why? Because the student's context is so different from that of his mentor. He believes that success is going to come by learning how to punch and kick. His mentor, being much wiser, begins the training in a very different way from what the boy expects.

In his thick Japanese accent, the mentor begins the first lesson by asking the boy if he is ready to begin.

"I guess so," says the boy.

The wise old mentor tells the boy to sit down so that they can have a talk.

"Walk on road right side, safe. Walk on road left side, safe. Walk on road middle, sooner or later, get the squish, just like grape. Here, karate same thing. You karate do 'yes' or you karate do 'no.' You do karate 'guess so,' sooner or later, get the squish, just like grape. Now ready?"

"Yes, I'm ready," says the student. And so they begin.

The mentor has a context. He knows that learning karate is a much more serious venture than his young student can imagine. To me it shows that the eagerness of a new student often overshadows his ability to think at a deeper level about where this new path will lead. It also shows how easy it is to get the squish. That's an important lesson for us to remember as investors, too.

"Either you learn to invest 'yes' or you learn to invest 'no.' You learn to invest 'guess so,' sooner or later you get the squish, just like grape"

Still, it takes the boy actually getting the squish a few times before he learns to accept the mentor's unorthodox training methods and realizes that learning karate will require his total commitment. His teacher invites him to enter into a sacred promise. The teacher's job is to teach the student to the best of his ability, and the student's job is to learn to the best of his ability and give his full effort.

The mentor emphasizes that the young boy will follow his instructions with no questions asked: "I say, you do. No question. Deal?"

"Deal," the boy answers.

The boy thinks he's going to be getting cool lessons on kicking and punching. He thinks he's going to learn a couple of slick moves and go back to those bullies in a few days and take them down.

To the young man's dismay, the first lesson has nothing to do with punching or kicking. Instead, the old man instructs the boy to wash several cars and wax them.

"Wax on, left hand. Wax off, right hand. Breathe in through nose, out through mouth. Very important." Immediately, the boy questions the methods of the teacher only to be reminded of their promises to each other: "I say, you do. No question."

Day after day, the boy is instructed to do various tasks that involve menial labor: waxing cars, painting fences, and sanding floors. With each passing day the boy becomes more frustrated because each day he arrives at the home of his mentor hoping to learn how to punch or kick.

Eventually the boy decides he wants to quit. At that moment the mentor shocks him by delivering a flurry of kicks and punches. The boy reacts instinctively and effectively blocks each punch and kick. By doing as his teacher has instructed, he has developed the muscle memory he needs to be able to defend himself without thinking. Waxing the cars, painting the fence and sanding the floors helped him learn and gain proficiency in a very natural way. He discovered and learned some things that were outside the traditional classroom through methods that he had never seen or experienced. Most importantly, his context dramatically improved. He was not only learning karate; he was becoming more mature. His philosophy began to change. His view of the world began to change and improve.

I smiled at the end of that movie, and I'll tell you, I wasn't the only one. When Daniel rears up into that crane move with his injured knee he triumphs over those bullies not just by being the better fighter, but by being the better person. He is completely transformed by his education with Mr. Miyagi. Education is transformation.

I know of no more powerful path to proficiency than when someone who is already proficient shows you the way. Even if you don't recognize the path they walk.

The Fog of Concern

When I finished reading *Rich Dad Poor Dad,* my wife and I were raring to go. We wanted to start out by investing in real estate. But we still had not changed our context. We were still focused on buying things more than learning things. We had a desire to be rich so we wanted assets on day one, but we had not yet shown proper respect for gaining our financial education. As a result, investing was very difficult for us in the beginning.

We looked at many houses and became frustrated by what seemed like a fog of concerns. It was as if we could not see what was a good investment and what was not. Every time we got close to making a move, we began to worry. *What if there's mold? It looks good, but I don't know anything about mold. What if I can't get a tenant? Worse yet, what if I do get a tenant and they trash the place? Why does the guy want to sell it so low? It seems like it's almost too good to be true, so there must be a reason why he wants to dump this on me.* Can you relate to this? I had a deep desire to buy assets, but I was shrouded in the fog of these concerns.

I wanted to call Robert (who I didn't know back then) and just yell, "Why couldn't you just print the address of the house I'm supposed to buy?!" Because that seemed like the answer—buy the right property, rent it out, sit back, and collect rent. Rinse and repeat until wealthy. If only Robert would tell me the right property to buy.

I didn't understand Rich Dad at all. I had missed the point completely.

But I didn't give up. I was determined to learn this stuff. I reread the book. What did Robert have that I didn't have? Duh. It was right on the cover in big yellow letters. He had a rich dad. He had a mentor.

My wife and I talked and changed our focus from looking for property to buy to looking for a mentor. And (go figure...) if that wasn't *exactly* what we found as soon as we started looking.

Mentors and Criteria Clear the Fog of Concern

My wife and I ran into an old basketball buddy of mine named Greg. We started catching up and I asked what he was doing these days, and lo and behold, he was a real estate investor. Now, if I hadn't changed my focus from finding property to finding *people*, that might not have even registered. But it did. He started talking, and my brain went...Bing! I started peppering him with questions. He was doing a couple deals a week buying residential properties, and had been in the business for about three years. From that I figured out three things: 1) if he'd been doing it that long, he must be more familiar with it than me, because he couldn't take on that much debt and survive without knowing what he was doing, 2) he had to have a money source other than a bank because no way could he finance stuff that quickly through traditional routes, and 3) he had to have a way to find these deals because I'd looked at dozens of houses and I hadn't bought one yet. So I knew he knew more than I did.

I was bold. I said, "Look, man, I'd really like to come to your office and just watch what you do."

He was kind of polite and changed the subject, but I just kept at him. I explained that I'd been trying to do real estate and was getting nowhere. I said, "Look, Greg, I just want to see, when you pick up the phone, I'm just curious who you call. Because I have a phone but I don't know who to call. And when you get in your car and drive somewhere, I want to see who an investor goes to see. Because I have a car but I have no idea who to go see. I just want to see what it is you do."

But I wasn't looking for a free ride. I didn't just want (or expect) to get all of his knowledge for free. In fact I paid him about $10,000 for teaching me how his system worked.

Now, Greg, he was organized. He had systems and criteria for analyzing a deal I had never thought of. But more than that, the day my wife and I came in, he said, "You're going to do a deal this week." He had a backer who didn't care who I was as long as I could bring him a good deal. That was the first key. His investor cared about the deal, not me or my credit. This was definitely not a bank.

With Greg's guidance, my wife and I found a good deal, got it in a foreclosure auction, refinanced it with a bank, and found a renter. We did it all with Greg standing beside us and showing us the way. There was no fog with Greg by our side. It all made perfect sense.

With Greg's help, my wife and I learned that investing has a lot to do with measuring an opportunity against certain criteria, and then matching it with a technique to harvest the cash flow. With his help, we had our very first income-producing asset! I shudder to think how long it would've taken me to learn any of that on my own.

Bonus Training!

Take a peek inside one of my own mentor meetings:

www.stockmarketcashflow.com

Today I still work with mentors of all kinds. I have mentors to help with learning paper assets. I have mentors for business. I have mentors for health and wellness.

There Are No Money Problems

As a final thought to this chapter on the importance of becoming a great student, I want to offer you a vital truth: *money comes from financial education*. You don't need to accept this right away, but you may someday come to realize that there are no true money problems—only education deficits. A lack of money is always secondary. It is never the primary problem.

As an investor, you'll find that education goals are vital because education is precisely where money comes from.

Like most people, I used to find myself falling into the trap of thinking that I had a money problem. I can think of times when I wanted to buy something big that would take more money than I had. In this type of situation, it is easy to think that a lack of money is the problem.

Equally dangerous is the old cliché, "It takes money to make money." This is a complete myth that needlessly stops many people from achieving their money goals. Money does not come from money; it comes from financial education.

Look again to some of our examples of financial success: Warren Buffett, Donald Trump, and Robert Kiyosaki. What if these men were stripped of all their money and assets today? What if they had to start over again with nothing? Would they remain poor or would they achieve success again? Of course they would find success. It's ridiculous to think they wouldn't. Their power comes from their education. The secret to their strength is their financial education. Their success comes from what they know, not from what they have.

Let's go back to the list of lifestyle goals people commonly list:

- I want to quit my job.
- I want to own a house on the beach.
- I want to own an exotic car.
- I want to travel the world.
- I want to be financially free.
- I want to help and serve others.

In my workshops, I ask my students: "Why don't you have these things already?"

No matter where in the world I ask this question, the answer is always the same, "Because I don't have enough money."

Never once, in any country, have I ever had a person reply, "Because I lack financial education."

When I speak with people who are struggling financially they usually see themselves as lacking money. None of them see the problem as a lack of financial education—at least not at first. Once we realize that financial education is where money comes from, we can change things.

This is great news because if a lack of money was really the problem that would be a pretty big obstacle. I don't have a Parable of the Money Tree for you!

While you can't choose to have people, governments, or employers give you more money, you *can* choose to get educated. You *can* choose to be a serious student and learn more about money. People who become obsessed with money wind up in a very different place than people who become dedicated to transforming themselves. Remember that education is transformation.

The Parable of the Orange Tree

When I was a child my grandma used to peel oranges for me. Whenever I smell citrus I think of her. She told me how oranges were full of vitamin C and how they'd make me healthy and help me grow big and strong. When I teach with Robert and the rest of the Rich Dad Advisor team we often use analogies to illustrate financial terms. My grandma and her oranges helped me understand derivatives.

Simply stated, vitamin C is a "derivative" of an orange.

If you want vitamin C every day, you'll probably become a hunter of oranges. But you'll quickly become frustrated at having to work so hard every day to find another bit of vitamin C for yourself. You will spend your time, talent, and energy seeking oranges. Some days you might find an orange, and some days you might not. You will likely live in scarcity.

A wiser solution might be to think about derivatives. Yes, vitamin C comes from the orange. But where does the orange come from? Of course, oranges come from orange trees. Instead of focusing on orange hunting, focus on growing your own orange tree. Find out the best seeds to get, the best soil to plant in—everything you'll need to ensure the most oranges from your tree. Now you have a plan for abundance. It's true that you might have to wait a season or two, but by focusing on the tree you will soon have more oranges than you can ever consume by yourself. In fact, your problem will be figuring out how to give your excess harvest away. You will live in abundance.

I like to also think of money as a derivative. Our lifestyle goals will depend on money, but where does the money come from? Just as oranges come from orange trees and a good harvest comes from learning about growing oranges, money comes from financial education. So you can take your current amount of time, your current amount of talent, and your current amount of ability and simply shift your focus.

Instead of focusing on money you can focus on learning where money comes from. Instead of focusing on the orange, you focus on the orange tree and growing oranges. Now you have a plan for abundance. It is true that you'll wait for a season when you focus on your financial education, but you'll have more money than you will ever be able to consume by yourself. Your greatest challenge might be figuring out how to give your excess money away. This is where Bill Gates is today. He left Microsoft because he needed to devote his time to the Bill and Melinda Gates Foundation and figure out the most effective ways to give his money away. That's not a bad place to be!

Chapter Summary

Let's review some of the important points of this first chapter:

1. We can discover new things in different ways than we learned in school.

   Learning does not need to be rigorous or difficult. In fact, learning is something our minds can do naturally and easily when we participate in the process. Discovery is a wonderful feeling; learning should be fun.

2. Context is about how we think.

   We can often learn about our context by paying attention to the questions we ask. Content is about the details, the how-to of a given task. Context is about the big picture, the *why* we are doing the task.

3. Use The Education Continuum.

   One of the most common mistakes to avoid is confusing awareness with proficiency. Set your educational goals within the context of The Education Continuum and know where you are in the process. It doesn't matter where you are on the Continuum at any given moment. It only matters that you are honest about where you are and that you have a plan to continue moving toward proficiency.

4. Learn by teaching.

   As you continue through the remaining chapters of this book, consider doing so with a pencil or pen and mark the sections that are particularly important to you and write down what you are learning so you can build on it as you go. Teach the things you discover to other people. This will help you remember more than if you simply read the book. Remember, you don't need to be an expert to share the things that you are learning.

5. Educational goals enable us to meet money goals set to achieve lifestyle goals.

   To improve your standard of living, you can set lifestyle goals. Those goals will have more meaning when you actually research how much money it will take to purchase your lifestyle goals. Once you've established your money goals you can look at different ways you can create that money by increasing monthly cash flow rather than by just saving and scrimping or loading up credit cards. You can set some educational goals even after you have graduated from high school or college. Educational goals should be specific ways of learning how to get more cash flow so that you can achieve your money and lifestyle goals.

6. Seek out and find mentors.

   As you focus your mind on investing, you'll begin to see things differently. You'll discover that some of the people you know and the people you need will become your allies. You will be on the lookout for mentors who can help you, and you'll be eager to invite them into your circle. In the process, you will also become part of their circle.

7. Money comes from financial education.

   Always remember the parable of the orange tree: Don't be an orange hunter, be an orange tree grower. Focus on your educational goals, and the money goals will follow naturally.

Chapter Two

Paper Assets in Your Wealth Plan

Building wealth is a matter of learning to buy or create assets intelligently and is part of a deceptively simple plan:

1. Get financial education.

2. Buy income-producing assets.

3. Build cash flow.

I'm a fan of Dr. Stephen Covey's *The 7 Habits of Highly Effective People*. If you've read the book, you might recognize that the above sequence of steps is a demonstration of at least two of the seven habits: begin with the end in mind, and put first things first. (If you haven't read the book, I highly recommend it. But remember: Don't just read it, study it.)

So if getting financial education is your first goal, then what kinds of things should you begin to study? As a serious student you might begin by studying all of the four income-producing assets classes:

Business
Real Estate
Commodities
Paper Assets

Please understand that different assets and asset classes have different advantages and pitfalls. It is vital to find a combination of assets that will suit your goals and strengths. You might find that you are best suited to focus on one type of asset, such as stocks. Maybe you have what it takes to be successful in business. Perhaps you'll find that real estate is what revs your engine. Or maybe you want multiple streams of income from all the assets classes. There is no right way, no one-size-fits-all answer, no magic bullet. The way that works for you might not work for your neighbor. But the more you know, the better equipped you'll be to put together the plan that *will* work for you.

To figure out what is best for you, you need at least a basic familiarity with all the asset classes. Only then can you find which combination will take you to your dream. Once you understand them, you can start to visualize how they will fit in the assets column of your balance sheet.

Let's get started by taking a brief look at the four asset classes.

Businesses

"Business" is a huge subject, but let's narrow it down to just two business topics: taxes and leadership. These are the two areas that most affect business as an asset.

The top financial liability for almost everyone is taxes. This is important to remember as we discuss creating a business as an asset. Growing up in the United States, I was taught about the important ideals of freedom: freedom of speech, of religion, and the right to own property.

I've heard it said that you can measure the amount of freedom you enjoy by how much of your stuff the government allows you to keep. I have a friend who likes to say that taxes are just a way for government to legally seize our property. If you choose not to pay your taxes, the government can seize the money from your bank account. And if you don't have money in your bank account, the government can seize your property.

If you're like me, your goal is to keep as much of your own money in your own pocket as possible. Reducing your tax burden is a good place to start taking positive action to make this happen.

Many countries offer tax structures with advantages and incentives to business owners. If you have not already done so, pick up a copy of Tom Wheelwright's book *Tax-Free Wealth* and you will see that the tax man is much kinder to educated business owners than to average working citizens.

Leadership also affects business as an incoming-producing asset. There are scores of computer programmer-types in the world, but Bill Gates of Microsoft and Steve Jobs of Apple stand out as exceptional leaders. They both left their university schooling to focus on their businesses.

Robert often talks about how "A" students wind up working for "C" students, and I've seen that in my own life. I've even lived it. It's funny how little grades and report cards matter once you're out in the real world. Leadership is a commodity that's much more valuable, and "A" students don't always make the best leaders.

Business is about organizing people and their talents. If you are a good leader, then business might be a great place for you. If you are a strong leader, then owning a business allows you to leverage the efforts of other people.

Think about this: An average person works eight hours a day, five days a week, 50 weeks a year. That's about 2,000 hours each year. Now let's suppose that as an employer you hire 100 people to work for you. Suddenly, you have 200,000 hours of effort working for you. You are able to magnify your efforts in a way that's impossible for a single person to accomplish on their own. Imagine what you could achieve if you had 200,000 hours at your disposal each and every year. Imagine the ways you could create cash flow and wealth for yourself!

OPEs

Business owners who are also good leaders benefit from what I call OPEs:

Other people's EDUCATION

Other people's EXPERIENCE

Other people's ENERGY

Other people's EFFORT

Other people's EXPERTISE

Other people's...EVERYTHING!

Think back to the S and B sections of the CASHFLOW Quadrant. What does it take to move from being an S, self-employed, to a B, a business owner? Think of the conductor of an orchestra. He never makes a sound himself. He is a leader. The moment he picks up a horn or a woodwind himself, he is no longer the conductor. In contrast, someone in the S quadrant is a one-man-band operating at his maximum capacity. He might be making lots of noise, but he simply cannot generate enough sounds to become a full orchestra on his own.

Another advantage of a business is that it can simply start as an idea. If a person builds a business plan with strong leadership, a strong mission, and a strong team, that person has created an asset. The business plan in and of itself can attract the people and capital to make it grow.

If you are a good leader and have a creative mind to solve problems, you might have what it takes to be a business owner. If you are resilient and good at raising capital and love bringing value to the lives of others, then you will likely enjoy business even though it is by far the most difficult of all the asset classes and has the lowest rate of success.

Real Estate

My friend Ken McElroy, Rich Dad Advisor for real estate, always mentions three things when he teaches real estate:

Partners - Financing - Management

I'll leave most of this to Kenny to explain on another day. But to make it simple, while business is about OPE, real estate is about OPM: Other people's money. It's about financing, management, partners, and structuring the deal—which is really all about going into debt. It's ironic that while most people are trying to stay *out* of debt, Kenny is actively trying to go into debt. (And it's working for him.) Like the fear of fire, many people are scared of getting burned by debt, so they prefer to stay away from the flames. But fire can be both good and bad. It can be used to heat your house or it can burn your house down.

Successful real estate investors like Kenny have replaced fear with respect. They study debt; they master it. They know the difference between good debt and bad debt

Real estate is attractive to many investors because it uses debt as a lever. It is a very popular way for someone to literally use other people's money to create cash flow and wealth.

If I go to a bank and ask for a loan for a business, they will typically have me jump through a series of hoops as they try to evaluate whether I'm worth the risk. Borrowing money for real estate, however, is a very different story. Banks or private investors will loan money for real estate because the real estate itself can act as collateral. If I'm not able to repay the loan, the bank will simply take back the property and sell it. That's why lending money on real estate is much less risky.

With real estate, the investor has control and can actually increase the value of the property, as well. It's one of the biggest advantages real estate has when compared to other assets, such as stocks. For example, if you buy an apartment building, you can renovate the building, update the appliances, raise the rents, and so forth. This is called *forced appreciation*. And the ways to do it are almost limitless.

Commodities

Commodities are about the hedge. Currency loses value; commodities retain value.

Commodities are used by investors in many ways. For example, you might receive monthly cash flow from your ownership in an oil well. Or you might receive a capital gain if you see a trend in the supply and demand of corn. You might buy some precious metals to hedge against a falling currency.

Commodities are those essential things we need in order to live, or the things we hold most valuable in society. So a person who owns commodities is in a position to trade. For example, if you own a lot of oil and people want to drive their cars, you have what they want. By owning an in-demand commodity, you are in a position of power.

If I have four strips of bacon and you have four eggs, we can trade with each other and both have breakfast without ever having to exchange regular currency. Currency is simply a way to make trading easier. But when a currency breaks down, we have to revert back to basic bartering.

How does this trading work? It's simple. You can take an ounce of gold anywhere in the world and trade it for things that you want or need. It's an in-demand commodity with real value. You trade that value for other things of value.

Paper Assets

This book focuses on the stock and options market. While there are other kinds of paper assets available to investors, we are limiting our discussion here to stocks and options.

A stock is a share of ownership in a company that is publicly traded on the stock market. The ownership of every publicly traded company is divided up into a specific number of these shares, and the number of shares is different for each company. So when you buy a stock, you are essentially buying a share of ownership in that company.

An option is the right to buy or sell a stock for a particular amount within a set amount of time.

Stocks Are Liquid

When investing in stocks, we can choose how we want to get profits. The two primary approaches are to seek capital gains (selling our stocks at a higher price than we paid for them) and to generate cash flow (creating new money). Seeking cash flow is my personal favorite because it allows me to control the situation better than just buying stocks. Either way, the stock market offers us the ability to easily buy and sell our paper assets.

By comparison, right now there are many people who would love to sell their real estate. But there's just one problem—not as many people can get the financing to *buy* real estate today. As an investor, when you face a situation where it's difficult to sell an asset because of market conditions, it is said that the asset lacks *liquidity*. Liquidity is the ease with which an asset can be converted to cash. It is important for us to consider the liquidity of an investment so we can always have a beneficial exit strategy. That's one thing you will love about the stock market—it generally offers investors good liquidity. If one of your stocks begins to go down, the market liquidity means you can sell it quickly before you have sustained a damaging loss. It also allows you to go from a good investment to a better investment in the blink of an eye.

Another advantage of liquidity is that a person doesn't need to have tremendous sales and negotiation skills. In business, those skills are vital. And developing those sales skills takes time and practice.

There's some irony to the liquidity of the stock market, because very few people actually take advantage of it. Many investors hold the same stocks and mutual funds year in and year out, and never think about selling a good stock for a better one or using any kind of exit strategy to maximize their profits. There is also a little hypocrisy here on the part of the big institutions that tell you to buy and hold. Stocks only fall when there are more sellers than buyers. While you are holding, the large institutions are often the ones selling!

Another thing to consider is that the liquidity of the market can bring an increase in volatility. The ability to buy and sell quickly can cause huge swings in supply and demand. Depending upon your situation and investing goals, this can be either a huge negative or a huge positive. There is not a one-size-fits-all answer. I predict there will be even more volatility in our market in the years ahead. But your investing strategy can use that volatility to your advantage.

Stocks Are Agile

When most people think about profiting from movement in the stock market, they think of one direction of movement: up. They don't understand the concept that stocks are agile. We can learn to profit from a stock no matter if it goes up, down, or sideways. That's very tough to do in business, but in the stock market, it doesn't matter—because there are profit strategies for movement in any direction. We will look at these strategies in detail in later chapters of this book.

Of all the asset classes, the stock market is probably one of the least difficult in which to earn a profit in relationship to the economy. When the stock market goes up we can buy stock, and when the stock market goes down we can short stocks. *Shorting* a stock is positioning yourself to make money when the price falls. If we use the stock market and the options market in harmony with each other, there are many income strategies that can provide cash flow even when the stock market is stagnant or going down.

Stocks Give Us the Ability to Scale

There is a common misconception that you need a lot of money before you can begin to invest. Perhaps that's why so many people put off their investing for so long. Some people never get around to it. Fortunately, investing in stocks allows almost anyone to begin their investing sooner rather than later.

Because buying stock is buying only a share of a company, buying stock is more affordable for the average person than buying an entire company or starting a business. But the beauty of this is that you can own exactly the same stocks as a famous investor like Warren Buffett. The difference is that, as a new investor, you'll probably buy a smaller number of shares than Buffett. A company you want to invest in may be a multi-billion-dollar enterprise, but you may be able to get a single share of its stock for just $25. The cost effectiveness of stock allows you to scale up into your investing as you gain the means to go bigger. For the average person, this is a faster way to invest than saving up for decades to purchase a franchise or some other business.

I frequently have students in my classes who love to talk about investing, but who have not yet actually bought any assets. They read a lot of investing books and listen to informative audio courses on building wealth. Yet their asset column is blank. They are making the mistake of waiting until they have a lot of money to begin investing. It's like the person who spends years reading every book they can find on how to play the piano, yet keeps putting off actually sitting down and playing a note. It's just not necessary. There is room for everyone at every level to sit down and play. Education is key, but remember that part of your education includes *doing* something.

Another avenue of profitable stock market investing is the options market. An *option* is the right to buy or sell a particular thing at a specified price within a set time frame. Just as we saw with stocks, options are also a very affordable way for anyone to begin their investing. As you advance in your knowledge and experience with options, you might be surprised to find just how much stock you can take control of for relatively small amounts of money and risk. In my view, this scalability is very attractive. It permits almost anyone to quickly place an asset on his or her financial statement. In fact, acquiring an asset with stocks can be done faster than any other asset class. Plus, the lessons learned from researching in the stock market are skills that will carry over into both real estate and general business. The stock market is a great place to learn about the concepts of exit strategy, hedging, and capital gains versus cash flow.

Leveraging with Debt

Like the real estate market, the stock market allows ample opportunity to use OPM. As stock investors we can take advantage of something that is called a *margin account*. Buying stock on margin allows you to leverage your money in a way that's a little different than how a real estate investor would use a bank loan. In my opinion, intelligently leveraging money with good debt is something that should be respected rather than something that should be feared. The debt that people should fear is debt that must be paid off by working at a job.

Leveraging without Debt

The options market offers us something more interesting than we can get with stocks alone. With options, we have the ability to leverage our money without going into debt at all. This type of leverage is very important because it can also act as something called a *hedge*. We will learn more about what hedges are and how you can use options to actually protect your stocks against loss in later chapters of this book.

One Asset Class Is Not Better than Another

One of the things you'll never hear me do is bash any particular asset class. I have often heard real estate teachers who bash the stock market and stock market teachers who bash the real estate market. Having a business is not "better" than owning real estate. Investing in real estate is not "worse" than investing in stock. Wise investors simply consider what they want to achieve with their investments, and then invest accordingly. I think many successful investors enjoy the diversification of owning assets across all the asset classes.

A person who invests exclusively in stocks is going to miss out on many of the tax advantages that the business owner will enjoy. A real estate investor may like the idea of having a portion of his wealth invested in assets that are liquid. An investor who believes the stock market will fall due to a bubble may be interested in exploiting that situation by seeking a capital gain that is available because of the agility of the stock market.

Here is a basic comparison table of what the different asset classes offer to investors. This table is not comprehensive, but it does illustrate the fact that investors can use different asset classes to achieve different investing goals:

Business	Real Estate	Paper	Commodities
Tax shelter	Effectively uses debt as a lever	Highly liquid	Tend to retain value
Other people's education	Investor can force appreciation	Agility to profit in up or down market	Hedge against inflation
Other people's experience	All transactions are negotiable	Scalable to invest large or small	Cash flow (own an oil well)
Other people's experterise	Pay back debt with cheaper dollars	Leverage with debt (margin)	Necessity of life (corn, wheat and other foods)
Other people's effort	Necessity of life	Leverage with no debt (options)	

Remember: this table doesn't show "better" and "worse" investment options. Instead, it shows you a simple comparison of just a few of the attributes of each asset class. Depending on your situation, liquidity can be good or bad. Being able to negotiate the price of an asset can be good or bad. Everything is relative. Everything is subjective.

BUILD ON IT

FOUNDATION	**Pick your asset classes: business, real estate, commodities, paper assets.**

Sometimes it's more important for you to ask new questions than to have new answers. Pause for a moment and consider which questions you are asking:

"What stock should I buy?"

Or... *"Where do paper assets fit into my overall financial plan, my financial statement?"*

The difference, of course, is your context. And that can make all the difference.

If we understand the various benefits and drawbacks of stocks, we will have an intelligent way of deciding how we can use them to achieve our investing goals. Conversely, the less a person understands about stocks the more likely a person is to fail when they use them in their strategy for investing.

Sales

If you're in business and you have inventory and you want to turn it back into cash, what do you need? Sales. If you have real estate and you want to cash out, what do you need? Sales. Not everyone likes putting on a smile and turning on the charm and making the sale. Stocks allow you to make sales without being a salesman. That's a huge advantage for a lot of people. Just click a button and...sold! I once had a business with a million dollars tied up in inventory. I guarantee there were days when I wished I could just click the mouse and make the sale. And I *like* sales.

While there is no good or bad asset class, business is my favorite because I am best suited to sales. I like people. Business is fun to me. That's the sandbox I like to play in. But I love the agility of paper. The stock market is the place I see where I can make money even if the economy completely crashes. There's a lot of fun in that too, let me tell you.

Chapter Summary

Let's review some of the important points of Chapter Two:

1. There is no "right" or "wrong" ("better" or "worse") when it comes to asset classes or investing options...it just depends what you enjoy and what fits into your investing strategy.

2. Wealth building is learning to buy assets intelligently.

   Wealth building is about making purchases and adding to the asset column of your balance sheet.

3. There are four primary classes of assets.

   You can expand the asset column of your balance sheet by adding any of these types of assets: businesses, real estate, commodities, and paper assets.

4. Business is about taxes and leadership.

   When you think about starting or buying a business, you can take advantage of tax laws. A business requires leadership. In business you'll be using other people's energy, other people's education, other people's experience, other people's effort, and other people's everything!

5. Real estate is about other people's money.

   The three most important things you can gain in your real estate education are: learning how to find and select the right partners, learning about creative financing, and learning about management. One of the great advantages of real estate is that it uses debt as a lever.

6. Commodities are about hedging.

   Commodities are those basic items that people want or need, such as corn, soybeans, pork bellies, oil, precious metals, lumber, and cotton. These items tend to retain their value because there is typically a strong demand for them, even when a currency fails.

7. Paper assets can be effective for all levels of investors.

   Most paper assets are liquid, which means they can be quickly and easily converted to cash. Paper assets are traditionally very agile and can be used to make money, no matter if the markets go up, down, or sideways. Paper assets also allow scalability, meaning that a person can begin with a very small investment. Some paper assets also allow for leverage without the use of debt.

To strengthen your understanding of these concepts, consider teaching them in your own words to a friend or family member. Good luck!

Chapter Three

Introducing the 4 Pillars of Investing

L et me introduce you to the 4 Pillars of Investing. As a student you will find that everything you will ever learn about making money with stocks will fit into one of these four pillars.

In Chapter Two we described wealth building as learning to buy or create assets intelligently. We also saw that the asset classes include business, real estate, commodities, and paper assets such as stocks and options. We learned that each asset class has its own language and nuances.

So how do you learn to buy these things intelligently? How do you make sound decisions when an opportunity presents itself? The answer is in learning the 4 Pillars of Investing. These pillars contain vital information for every type of investor in any asset class, and they are vital whether you are investing for capital gains or cash flow.

In preparing to write this book, I sat down and reviewed everything I had learned from my mentors and teachers about investing. I realized that everything I knew fit very nicely into four categories:

1. I had learned about studying entities (Fundamental Analysis).

2. I had learned how to study trends (Technical Analysis).

3. I had learned techniques to position myself for profit (Cash Flow).

4. I had learned about managing risk (Risk Management).

These categories make up what I call my 4 Pillars of Investing. When you dedicate yourself to studying these four pillars you will learn the criteria that will allow you to look at any investment opportunity in any asset class and make better decisions. These four pillars will support your financial education goals. You will learn to buy assets intelligently and build wealth.

So let's get started by looking at Pillar #1.

Pillar 1: Fundamental Analysis

Fundamental analysis examines the strength of an entity. We need to be able to tell the difference between an entity that is strong and an entity that is weak, be that entity a private company, a charity, even a nation. And we do that by looking at the financial statements. The financial statement tells us the strength of the entity.

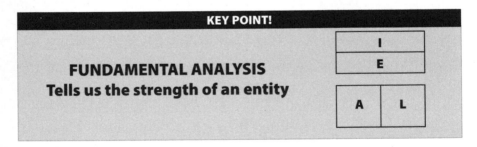

My college basketball coach was a master when it came to teaching fundamentals. His teams won many championships, and he was well known among avid college basketball fans. People often ask me why I think he was so successful. My answer is always the same: He absolutely demanded perfection in the parts of the game that don't require talent, but do require tremendous effort. Not everyone has the same level of talent, but we all can give supreme effort. There are certain parts of the game that are basic at any level, be it high school or the pros. To have success, you must become proficient in them. My coach was obsessed with the fundamentals, and he coached them well.

The same rigor in fundamentals is needed for financial success, and basic rules apply to every entity—from sovereign governments to corporations to individuals. There are certain financial fundamentals that must be in line for any entity to flourish. In this chapter, you will begin to understand what these fundamentals are. You will also discover how to compare one entity to another and immediately know which one is in a stronger financial position.

Fundamental analysis is the process of looking at some basic numbers and evaluating the financial strength of the entity based on those numbers. I'm going to help you discover what those numbers mean and where you can find them. You're going to discover that as you learn more about how to look at these fundamental numbers you will have an increased ability to make wise investment decisions. You'll be able to set a bar for comparison and then quickly see if the opportunity measures up with your expectation of a good investment.

One helpful way to look at fundamental analysis is to think of it as going to the doctor for a checkup. To analyze your condition, the doctor begins with the basics. She's probably not concerned with the color of your hair or the color of your eyes. These things don't tell the doctor very much about how healthy you are. But she will check your blood pressure and your pulse. She'll tap you on the knee to see if your reflexes are responding properly. She'll use a stethoscope to listen to the beat of your heart and the sound of your lungs. She'll write down your "vital signs." These vital signs represent the fundamental state of your basic health. Collecting and analyzing these numbers is the doctor's first step in figuring out what's happening with your overall system.

When it comes to analyzing a nation's economy or your own financial standing, conducting a fundamental analysis as the first step will give you a quick understanding of financial fitness to see if everything is in order. The financial vital signs can tell us a lot about the health of the entity.

Fundamental analysis also helps us determine value. The more financially healthily the entity, the more valuable it is in the marketplace.

Fundamental analysis is a critical tool for leaders of all kinds. It can be used to discover weakness and, in turn, guide policies for improvement, whether it is being used at the highest levels of government or a for couple at the head of a household. It is a very valuable diagnostic tool.

As we study fundamentals you will learn:

1. How to measure the financial strength of any entity

2. How to see the value of the entity

3. How to diagnose causes of weakness

4. How to change policies to fix weakness and predict change

5. How to see the two sides of any transaction and identify the winner and the loser

6. Why it seems that investors can predict the future

Now, those are things I wish I could have learned in school!

BUILD ON IT

**PILLAR #1
Fundamental analysis tells
us the strength of an entity.**

Pillar 2: Technical Analysis

The second of the four pillars is called technical analysis—"technicals" for short.

Technicals are the story of supply and demand in pictures. Supply and demand creates trends.

TECHNICAL ANALYSIS
Tells us the trend

Picture yourself as the owner of a golf course. You've done a great job with every part of your business. Your course is one of the best golf properties anywhere in the world. In fact, there are so many people who want to play on your golf course that there's no way you can accommodate everyone. You have earned the luxury of being in high demand. As a result, tee times on the course are in short supply.

What does this mean to your business? Now you can charge more than your competitors because there's a higher demand for a tee time at your course than anywhere else. On your computer you have a chart that shows the history of your prices as they've climbed year after year. Using this trend, you can forecast where your prices are likely to be in the future. This process of examining a chart and projecting what you expect to happen in the future is called *technical analysis*.

When you buy a share of stock in a company, it makes sense that you will want to carefully examine at least two things:

1. Since you're going to own a share of the company, it feels very natural to want to know how strong the company is financially and how it stacks up against other companies when it comes to the basic numbers (or *fundamental analysis*).

2. You want to see how eager other investors are to buy shares in the company and if there's a high demand for the shares that could drive the company's stock price higher and higher (or *technical analysis*).

It is very important to understand trends because you will see that, with the stock market, opportunity is always present. In the section on technical analysis you will learn:

1. Rules to identify a trend

2. How to read the story the trends are telling

3. That investors use patterns to determine what is most likely to happen next

4. How the use of technical tools helps investors find opportunities and see warnings

BUILD ON IT

PILLAR #2
Technical Analysis examines the supply and demand (trends) of a stock.

Allow Discovery to Happen

The first two chapters of this book introduced you to the idea of *context*. Those discussions were designed to help open your mind so you can begin to think differently. Now you can feel that we are beginning to move into *content* and some of the important how-to's of investing.

At this point, I want you to give yourself permission to learn about fundamental analysis and technical analysis in a different way. If you do this, your experience will be more fun and enlightening right from the beginning. Here are a few suggestions to keep in mind as you dig into the chapters on fundamental and technical analysis:

Move at Your Own Speed

Unlike school there's no test at the end of the week, there's no grade, so there's no pressure for you to learn everything completely and perfectly the first time you see it.

I remember in college I had to take an organic chemistry class. The material was very complex. But what compounded the problem was that I had to learn it so quickly. I felt pressure because I had to understand everything that was being presented the first time. The stress was brutal and not conducive to really learning the subject. I started to panic because the penalties for not understanding things were so severe and so immediate. I could become ineligible to play ball if I failed the test. It was hard to think of anything but that consequence.

Even after college I found myself reacting the same way, out of habit. If I was in a situation where I didn't understand a concept quickly when it was given to me I became tense, nervous, and stressed out. Now I have learned to relax and let things come to me at my own pace, but it took changing my context. By taking the pressure off, learning has now become one of my favorite activities.

So when you study the chapters on fundamental and technical analysis, please allow yourself—remind yourself—to relax. I'm confident you will do just fine. If you ever do feel anxiety, let that be a signal to take a breath...and relax. Remind yourself that it's okay to read the material more than once, and it's okay to slow down.

I still remember the lesson I learned from a teacher as she used the analogy of learning to drive a car with a manual transmission. We can surely move from ignorance to awareness to competency on the Education Continuum simply by listening to someone else explain the process of letting out the clutch and pushing the accelerator pedal. But proficiency comes when we're actually trying to follow the instructions by sitting in the driver's seat and trying to operate the car. When we try to put those concepts into action, we will inevitably stall the car. But it's not that big of a deal because stalling the car is part of the process. That's how you learn to drive a car with a manual transmission. We learn by making mistakes.

After several attempts, you begin to get the feel of it. You learn how to make tiny adjustments until you get to the point where you can shift from gear to gear, listen to the engine, and know when to up-shift or down-shift,—and even gently balance the clutch and brake when starting on a hill. Before long, you're driving that car without even thinking about it. You have arrived at proficiency.

And just because you stall the car, it doesn't mean you're not learning. I stalled the car when my dad was teaching me. Will I teach my sons the exact same way? You bet I will. It's still the best way to teach. Killing the engine is just part of the process. No harm will come to my sons; I'll be sitting there right next to them until they get the hang of it.

So please remember there's no need to put pressure on yourself as you learn these investing concepts. Take a breath and enjoy the discovery. Once you've built your investing foundation with these first two pillars, it will be time to move on to the third pillar, which is certainly the most exciting one to an investor: cash flow.

Pillar 3: Cash Flow Strategies

Once we see the strength of a company (fundamentals), and the trend of the market (technicals), we then decide how we want to position ourselves to profit.

> **KEY POINT!**
>
> **CASH FLOW**
> **Is about your position in the market:**
> **up, down or sideways**

Some investors put themselves in the position of aiming to profit from a capital gain, which means buying low and selling high, like when you buy and sell a house. Others aim to place themselves in a position of cash flow, like renting a house. To understand one strategy, it helps to understand the other.

The term *cash flow* certainly gets everyone's heart beating a little faster. Ultimately, that's what we really want as investors. Because as money freely flows into your account through smart investment decisions, you will experience what true freedom feels like. The goal of this book is to help you begin to feel confident and comfortable in your ability to draw cash from the stock market on a regular basis—no matter the direction in which the market moves. That's the beauty of it: You'll learn how this can be done in markets that go up, down, or sideways.

Cash Flow Is a Solution to the Problem of Expenses

Everyone has expenses like food, clothing, shelter, taxes, and recreation, among many others. Expenses are the basic financial problem of life. We can solve that problem in one of four ways:

Employee

Self Employed

Business Owner

Investor

If you need $5,000 each month to solve your expense problem, then to move from the left side of the quadrant to the right side, your financial statement must change from this:

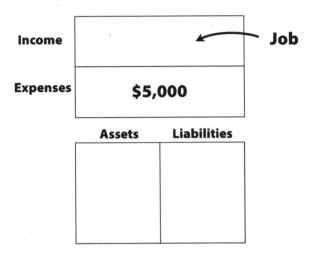

to this:

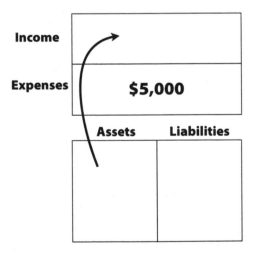

The Best Cash Flow Is Not Dependent on Bull Markets

Many people who work at a job put money away into some sort of a contribution retirement program such as a 401(k) or an individual retirement account (IRA). The money put into these accounts finds its way into the stock market through mutual funds or unit trusts, depending on the country in which you live. Whether or not you make money is often directly dependent upon the performance of the overall stock market. Due to the fact that these strategies are almost entirely focused on the long term, they are not a source of current cash flow for the investor. But here's the problem: The stock market doesn't always (or only) move in a steady upward direction. It can—and definitely does—travel upward, or downward, or remain stagnant for long periods of time.

In the United States the predominant account for retirement investments is called a 401(k). Unfortunately, the value of these investments is dependent on a bull market. So rather than being designed to grow cash flow, they are designed to grow net worth. As the market fluctuates, so does net worth.

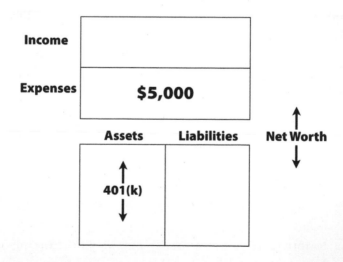

When I think about 401(k) accounts they remind me of Aesop's fable about the goose that laid golden eggs. Most contribution retirement plans rely on money earned in the past (what I call "old money") to solve expense problems in the future.

GOLDEN GOOSE
Generates "new money"

GOLDEN EGG
Relies on "old money"

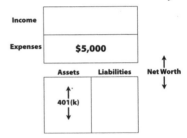

The plans that rely on old money are in a risky situation. Instead of having monthly cash flow that could last indefinitely, the investor is left with what feels like two hour glasses. One is filled with money and the other with time. That's why one of the main fears people have is running out of money in retirement. This wouldn't happen if they knew how to generate "new money."

I want to introduce you to a totally new way of thinking—one you may never have considered before. These new "golden-goose" ideas are different from what you experience when you let your money sit in long-term retirement accounts.

When it comes to purchasing stocks, fundamental analysis is the process of gathering information about the strength of a company, and technical analysis is the process of gathering information about the supply and demand for that stock. When you have that information, you can use it to determine whether you're investing your money in a golden goose or a golden egg. You're going to discover there are a variety of ways to *harvest* what you see in fundamental and technical analyses.

In the chapters on cash flow strategies you're going to see some examples of how to turn this information into potential profit, as well as some of the rules that we follow when we execute a certain investing strategy. I'm also going to give you some insight into how to choose one strategy over another and some methods to give you confidence in the decisions you make to help you move toward your money and lifestyle goals.

Learning many different cash flow strategies is like having many different colors available to you when painting a picture. With a variety of colors in front of you, think of how much more effectively you can mix and match those colors to help that painting match your vision of what you want it to be.

To their detriment, many investors develop fundamental and technical criteria that limit them only to capital gains. Moreover, many limit their toolbox to bullish strategies only. As a college athlete, I had to learn many different offensive schemes and had many plays in my playbook that could address many different situations. I would take what the defense gave me and find ways to win, no matter what.

The same can be said of taking what the market gives you—be it a trend up, down, or sideways—and addressing it.

By learning different ways to position yourself for cash flow (or even a capital gain, for that matter), you are beginning to understand that there are opportunities for profit no matter what the market does.

Some of what you will learn in the section on Cash Flow:

1. How to get a capital gain when the market goes up

2. How to get a capital gain when the market goes down

3. How to get leverage without using debt

4. How the stock and option markets can work together to generate cash flow

BUILD ON IT

PILLAR #3
Cash Flow is about choosing a position in the market.

Pillar 4: Risk Management

Whether you invest in real estate, stocks, or any other asset class, you have to remember: Things can change suddenly.

KEY POINT!

RISK MANAGEMENT
Helps us deal with uncertainty or when we're just plain wrong.

If the market crashes and your retirement is lost, do you have a plan B?

If you save money and the dollar crashes, what will you do?

If there is a flood and your home is lost, do you have insurance?

No matter what you do, there are always some things that are beyond your control and others you can always control. Risk management is using the things you can control to deal with those you can't. I can't control the flood, but I can control whether or not I buy insurance.

The Relationship Between Risk and Control

You might want to pause for a moment and consider this key point: Risk is related to control.

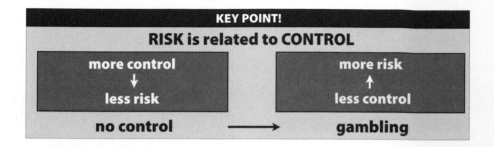

Whenever someone is about to invest money or use debt as an investment lever, they would be wise to consider how much control they have over the outcome of the investment. The question of control is equally important for people who have placed large amounts of money into traditional retirement plans that are broadly diversified across the markets. How much control do they have over the outcome? It is a sobering question to consider.

An investor has no control over the first two pillars we discussed, fundamental analysis and technical analysis. When we look at a company's numbers, we understand that its performance is beyond our control. We don't make the day-to-day decisions inside the company. We are not out there selling its products. We may own some shares of the company, but we have little to no impact on company policy. Likewise, when we look at the chart of that company's stock and see the trend of the share price of the stock, we realize that the direction of the stock price is beyond our control as well.

No matter how badly you might want the price of the stock to go up, it's completely out of your control. The same is true with the company's earnings. We can't control these things any more than we can control the weather or the lottery.

Remember that the first two pillars, fundamental analysis and technical analysis, are about gathering and analyzing information—not about controlling that information.

BUILD ON IT

**PILLAR #4
Risk management is using what you can control to deal with what you can't.**

Things You Can Control

After you've gleaned some vital information by conducting a fundamental analysis (looking at the financial strength of a company) and technical analysis (looking at the supply and demand for that stock), it's time to consider a cash flow strategy and how you want to manage the risk associated with that strategy. Again, you have no control over the first two pillars. But you have total control and full responsibility for your actions with the last two pillars.

In other words, you really can't control what the weather's going to be, but you do get to choose how you'll deal with it. You can't control a hurricane that's coming your way. But if you gather information that shows a hurricane is coming, you can benefit from that information and begin selling emergency supplies to those who need them. You can also manage your risk by purchasing insurance to protect your own home. These actions are entirely up to you. The same is true with your cash-flow investing.

You also control the level of your financial education. In Chapter One we discussed the importance of investors becoming serious students. It is entirely up to you how far you want to go with each of the 4 Pillars of Investing. That's very good news. Because if we realize that our lifestyle goals are related to our money goals, and that our money goals are achieved when we reach our education goals, then the 4 Pillars of Investing become a clear pathway to success. We now know what to study and what to work on. We know how to grow our very own orange trees with endless supplies of delicious fruit.

Some of what you will learn in the section on risk:

1. You will learn about many different kinds of risks investors face.

2. You will expand your financial vocabulary.

3. You will learn about exit strategies.

4. You will learn about hedges.

5. You will learn about position sizing.

The 4 Pillars in the Education Continuum

Paper assets are a great place to start learning the 4 Pillars because of its advantage in scalability and liquidity. But it would be a grave mistake, for example, to think that real estate investors do not need to understand technical analysis in their day-to-day business. I have heard Rich Dad Advisor Ken McElroy declare many times that his real estate business is a trend business. The 4 Pillars offer a foundation for any financial education.

Now that you have a basic understanding of each of the four pillars, it's time to become more *aware* of what they are. It's time to begin to become more *competent* in each pillar. As you desire to become more competent, your mind will automatically search for mentors and ways you can practice to become more and more *proficient* because of the law of attraction. Because this is simply how your brain works naturally.

The Education Continuum™

Ignorance → Awareness → Competency → Proficiency

Focusing on your education goals more clearly identifies the people and the opportunities that will help you achieve your goals. This increased focus and desire to identify solutions will give you the feeling that these people and opportunities are being drawn to you.

As you study the 4 Pillars of Investing, I encourage you to think about your progress in each pillar along the Education Continuum. It's a good way to evaluate where you are in your learning. There's a big difference between being aware of what a financial statement is and being proficient in conducting a fundamental analysis of that statement. There's a big difference between being aware of technical analysis and being proficient in reading stock charts. The process of moving toward proficiency in the Education Continuum is even more important with the last two pillars: cash flow and risk management. Because this is where your decisions and actions will directly impact your profits.

Cash flow strategies and risk management are double-edged swords: You can do the most good for yourself, but also the most harm. As investors, our goal is proficiency with these pillars. As you take this journey, enjoy the discovery of each pillar and remember that success is the natural order of things. Just let it happen.

Chapter Summary

Let's review some of the important points of Chapter Three:

1. Fundamental analysis helps us know the **financial strength of an entity.**

   A financial statement reveals the financial fitness of an entity. You can use those numbers to see its value, diagnose its problems, and better forecast the future.

2. Technical analysis helps us **identify trends.**

   By reading stock charts we can identify trends. We can see changes in supply and demand. We can see patterns that tell us what is likely to happen next. We can see warning signals in the market.

3. Cash Flow strategies are how we choose to **position ourselves to profit.**

   Learning all the cash flow and capital gain strategies gives you the opportunity to take what the market gives you and have profit potential in any market—be it up, down, or sideways—instead of being at its mercy.

4. Risk management is about **dealing with the unexpected.**

   Every serious investor needs countermeasures to deal with the unexpected or to protect themself when they're wrong.

5. The 4 Pillars are not just for stock investors, they are for **all investors**.

   No matter the assets class, proficiency in the 4 Pillars makes for better decision-making!

Chapter Four

Pillar 1: Fundamental Analysis

When you buy stock you become an owner of the company. It makes sense then that if you are an owner, you should have a good idea about the financial condition of your company. That's why the first step on your journey toward generating reliable capital gains and cash flow from your investments is to learn about fundamental analysis.

Again, fundamental analysis is the process of looking at certain numbers to determine the health of an entity. The numbers you look at to determine that health are found on the financial statement.

It doesn't matter if the entity is a person, a family, a church, a company, a school, or even a nation. And it all begins with the financial statement. By looking at a financial statement, I can see the whole sum and substance of an entity. I can see its strengths and weaknesses. I can compare it to any other entity. I can do this for an organization with money flowing through it. I can do it for an entity on the verge of economic collapse. The whole story is in the numbers.

Financial statements tell us what we need to know about a business without ever setting foot in that business. They tell us what we need to know about a charity, even if we don't know its values or mission. They tell us what we need to know about a country without us ever knowing anything about its politics. They tell us about a family...without the need to ever meeting them.

A financial statement is the heart and soul of fundamental analysis

In the Rich Dad series of books there are a lot of references to financial statements. Many of the stories that Robert tells are about the lessons from his rich dad, lessons triggered by Robert showing him his financial statements. Rich dad didn't need to physically visit Robert's business for an on-site inspection. He didn't need to know all about the products or who was on the management team. Yet Robert's rich dad was able to make a quick and accurate evaluation about the strength of the business. "Your business has financial cancer," rich dad would sometimes say to Robert. He could make that evaluation by looking at the company's financial statement and nothing more. When he looked at the financial statement and made his prognosis, rich dad was conducting a *fundamental analysis*. Now it's time for you to learn to do the same thing.

Below is a picture of a financial statement that most every student with the Rich Dad context is familiar with. We'll be using pictures like this throughout the book, so let's have a look at it and see what it means.

The Income Statement

You can divide a basic financial statement into two simple parts that anyone can understand. There's the income statement, where we show the income (I) coming in and the expenses (E) going out. When you write a check, that money is going out of your account as an expense. When you deposit a paycheck or a dividend check, that is money coming into your account as income. With these two numbers we can easily calculate *cash flow*—simply by subtracting the *expenses* from the *income*. As you will see, sometimes cash flow is positive and sometimes it is negative.

Cash Flow = Income - Expenses

The Balance Sheet

The second half of the financial statement is a balance sheet. Traditionally, the asset column (A) is the list of all the things you own, and shows how much all those things are worth. As you probably know by now, in the Rich Dad world we also expect our assets to provide us with income. The liability column (L) is a list of how much you owe and to whom. Simply put, let's say that assets put money in our pocket and liabilities take money out.

From there, we add up the value of all the assets and subtract our total liabilities. The resulting number is the *equity*. Sometimes you will hear people refer to equity as *net worth*.

Equity = Assets - Liabilities

People who have a limited financial education will often crow about their net worth and ask you about yours. But as you will soon see, net worth is typically an overrated number and is much less important than cash flow.

At this point we have our first six numbers to use in our fundamental analysis:

1. Income

2. Expenses

3. Cash flow

4. Assets

5. Liabilities

6. Equity (net worth)

Did you see how simple that was? With just a little basic math, we are able to generate those numbers.

BUILD ON IT

The heart of any fundamental analysis is the financial statement.

The most important number so far is cash flow, of course. If we are analyzing a sovereign nation, the cash flow situation will tell us if that country's government is financially solvent or not. For a company, the cash flow number helps us understand if the company is currently making money. And for an individual, the cash flow helps us understand if that person is living within their means.

Let's look a little deeper into these three types of financial statements:

Personal

Corporate

Sovereign

You can easily get a basic understanding of these statements without an accounting degree. At this point, we're not interested in going through every little detail with a fine-tooth comb. By understanding just a few basic numbers, you will be able to make a quick overall assessment of any of these types of entities just like rich dad could.

The Relationship Between Financial Statements and Policy

There's a law in physics that says the velocity of a body remains constant unless the body is acted upon by an external force. It sounds like fancy language from Einstein or some PhD, but what it means is that if something is standing still, it has to get smacked to make it move, and if something is moving, it has to get smacked to change its direction. That's called a force.

In the world of economics, one of the most powerful forces is any kind of policy made by a government. A policy is simply a decision that leads to a course of action.

KEY POINT!

Why does a financial statement look the way it does? POLICY!

It's amazing to see how a few words issued by a government as policy can have a massive impact on its financial status. For example, the terrorist attacks inflicted on the United States on September 11, 2001 were horrific events. They also had an impact on the financial health of the country. The truth is that these attacks and events like them have much less of an impact than the country's policies. It was actually the fiscal policies that set the stage for and, possibly, triggered the financial crisis that overtook the United States and much of the world.

Today's uncertain and turbulent financial situation is clearly the result of foolish and undisciplined fiscal and monetary policies introduced by the Congress and Federal Reserve in the wake of 9/11. Their policies left all of us seriously exposed to potential trouble.

Former Comptroller General David Walker has said:

> "I would argue that the most serious threat to the United States
> is not someone hiding in a cave in Afghanistan or Pakistan, but
> own our fiscal irresponsibility."

Financial hard times have come and gone throughout history. They occur from time to time in every society. But what can a person do to weather these financial storms? What can a business do? And what can a government do?

When a person, a company, or a government declares bankruptcy it is often a result of poor policy. And it's often the consequences of those earlier policy decisions that are now affecting them in very troubling ways. On the other hand, those who are able to survive these storms are typically those who have made solid financial policies. Their decisions have placed them in a good enough position to absorb getting smacked without being pushed seriously off course.

In the next few pages you are going to discover for yourself that policy is the strongest factor influencing any financial statement. You will also see that the fastest way to improve a financial statement is to improve the policies that support it. When I hear stories of Robert's rich dad giving him candid and often severe feedback, he was really critiquing Robert's business practices—his corporate policies. It was these policies that caused problems that appeared in the financial statement. Robert often does the same for me today, and I welcome his feedback.

BUILD ON IT

The financial statement is a reflection of policy.

The relationship between policy and fundamental analysis is inseparable. A weakness in a financial statement points to weakness in policy. Hence, the B-I Triangle, which illustrated the 8 Integrities of a Business, is built around having a passionate mission, capable leadership, and a strong team.

Robert writes extensively about the B-I Triangle. It's a diagram his rich dad used to teach him about the eight critical elements, or integrities, that make up a business. If any of these elements are weak, the business is destined for failure. If any are having problems, those problems will likely show up as weak numbers on the financial statement.

It is the leaders, the team members, and the mission that dictate policy. Adherence to that policy, be it good or bad, will determine what the financial statement will look like.

We are going to start our study of fundamental analysis by looking at the policies that affect sovereign nations. When it comes to sovereign nations, the strength or weakness of their financial statements is the result of fiscal and monetary policies.

Sovereign Fundamental Analysis

I spend a lot of my time focusing on sovereign fundamentals. The reason is simple: I believe that everything that happens financially at both the corporate and personal levels often occurs under the umbrella of the health of sovereign nations. The policies they are making, and the consequences of those policies, affect us every single day.

My home country is the United States, so let's begin by doing a basic fundamental analysis on the U.S.A. at the time I was writing this book. These numbers, of course, will change over time. But regardless of where the numbers go in the future, this process will show you how you can do a sovereign fundamental analysis for yourself at any point in time. What's important is the understanding of how to conduct a fundamental analysis and read a financial statement.

Sovereign Fundamental Analysis and Fiscal Policy

There are two types of policy that affect sovereign fundamentals: *fiscal* and *monetary*. In the case of United States, you're going to find that many of the problems we see with the numbers on the financial statements are due to foolish fiscal policy.

Fiscal policy refers to how a government chooses to spend its money. The ugly numbers we will uncover have little to do with bad luck or unforeseeable events. We're also going to view this policy in light of some demographics to determine what the future will bring.

Fiscal Policy

In the United States, *fiscal policy* is set by Congress. The words *politics* and *policy* refer to the decisions made by those who are in positions of power. The United States Congress has many powers. But when it comes to fiscal policy, it has two fundamental and obvious powers that have and will have an impact on the nation's financial statement:

1. Congress can raise or lower taxes.

2. Congress can increase or decrease spending.

This means that much of how the financial statement of the United States looks is determined by Congress and its fiscal policy. Congress will determine income by tax policy. It will determine expenses by the budget. Taxes and spending can create a surplus or a deficit. If there is a deficit, Congress may be required to borrow to cover the shortfall, forcing it to increase debt.

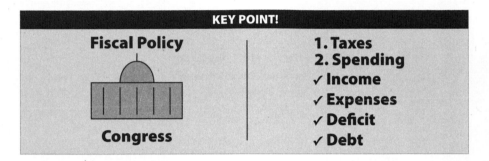

Let's break all that down piece by piece. Republicans and Democrats, influenced by their respective special interest groups, create legislation and submit a budget for the country. The Tax Code is a list of the laws that require people and corporations to pay taxes. The United States Internal Revenue Code contains thousands of pages of tax policy. As we begin to assemble a financial statement for the U.S. government, we can begin by putting taxes in the income column so that it looks like this:

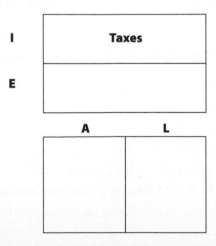

The U.S. government's spending activities are very complex. Income generated through taxes is spent on a variety of things including military, public roads and infrastructure, education, entitlement programs, debt payments, and more. All of this spending gets added up and put in the expense column like this:

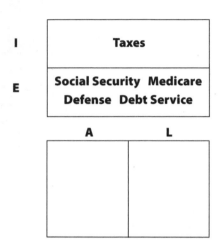

Next, we're ready to talk about *gross domestic product* (GDP)—perhaps the largest asset of the United States. The explanation I want to give you is a little different from standard accounting practices and approaches it from the Rich Dad perspective we mentioned earlier: assets put money in our pockets. The opposite of this, of course, reminds us that liabilities take money out of our pockets. Remember, this is not an accounting lesson. Instead, this discussion is designed to help you understand what's happening from a fundamental viewpoint.

Let's start by understanding what gross domestic product actually means. It's an important financial term for your investing vocabulary. GDP is used to describe the amount of goods and services a country produces during a given year. All of these goods and services are totaled together and given a dollar value, which we call GDP.

Since the U.S. GDP is the value of all the productivity of the United States, let's put it into our financial statement in the asset column. This is accurate in the sense that the nation is only as strong as its people and corporations, and the value they produce.

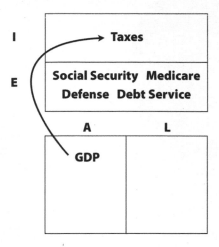

As the people and the corporations of the country earn money, shown as GDP, the government takes a portion of that money as taxes. This makes GDP a vital part of our sovereign fundamental analysis. It's the engine that produces money that the government can tax.

All of taxes and spending are dependent on the size of the GDP. Let's visualize the GDP as a big pizza. Congress gets to take a slice out of that pizza in the form of taxes. As long as that pizza stays large, then the government is satisfied with that slice. But what happens if one day the pizza shrinks? Suddenly, the government's slice isn't as large as it was before. And if the government has to continue taking a smaller slice of a smaller pizza for several years in a row, then it gets really hungry. That period of time—the years when the pizza is smaller—is known as a *recession*.

When GDP shrinks, and the size of the government's slice shrinks, Congress faces a real problem: It doesn't collect as much as it expected in taxes. When the citizens and the corporations are producing less, they usually earn less. With less money being earned, the total amount of taxes collected drops. As a result, the income of the nation gets smaller. This is what we see in a recession.

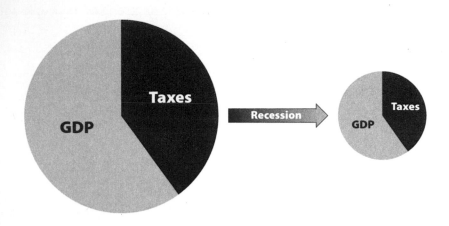

You may be wondering why this is a problem for Congress. It can just hurry and cut spending to match the lower tax income, right? Well, it's not that easy. Governments are known for making future promises to their citizens. Once they make these promises, it's not easy to get out of them.

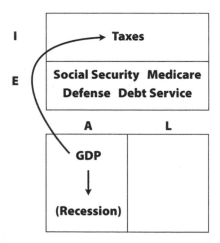

Let's look at some of the promises made by the United States and how difficult it is to modify them quickly when tax income is drastically reduced.

When the government commits to a war, it's a very expensive action. Moreover, there is seldom a clear end date for a war. You can't just stop fighting one day when the money runs out. And when the government promises citizens that it will pay for their Social Security and Medicare benefits, they need to fulfill those promises. And at any given moment, the country has road construction underway and other infrastructure improvements that need to be finished. There are countless government offices that need to stay open to serve its citizens. And the U.S. government has taken on a lot of debt, and it needs to pay that back as well—or at least keep making payments on that debt.

Just because the breadwinner of a household loses his or her income-producing job, the expenses of life don't stop piling up. The family still needs to eat, have clothing, and have a roof over their heads. It's the same for a country.

However, in a situation where income is suddenly lower than expected, individuals usually behave very differently compared to a government. When the government's tax income is reduced, it has the power to change policy and take a bigger percentage of our money than it did before. Congress might feel pressure to raise taxes in order to make up for the decline in tax income. Of course, it can also make decisions to cut its spending. But with so many people contributing to those decisions, and so many points of view, the fight over what cuts to make can get ugly in a hurry.

This is a good time for us to look at the government's cash flow for some additional insights. Remember, cash flow is calculated by subtracting expenses from income. For the government, it looks like this:

Cash Flow = (Taxes Collected) – (Government Program Expenses)

If the tax income is greater than the amount of government spending, we call it a positive cash flow or a *surplus*. However, if the government spending is greater than the tax income, we call it a negative cash flow or a *deficit*.

You probably already know the difference between a surplus and deficit. The reason I have decided to address this simple and basic topic is that I'm continually shocked by the number of people I teach around the world who do not know the difference between *debt* and *deficit*. A debt is simply a promise to pay. A deficit is a shortfall. It's a massive difference, and one you need to understand sooner rather than later.

Suppose your dog becomes sick and you take it to the veterinarian. That is an unexpected expense, and it might cause you to have a shortfall that month. If you have enough money in your bank account to cover the bill, you can simply cover the shortfall (deficit) that month by writing a check. However, if you don't have extra money in your bank account, you might have to put that expense on your credit card. This means you promise to pay back the bank later (debt) for that visit to the vet now.

If the government has a lot of money in the Treasury, it doesn't really worry about a little deficit spending. It will just use money in the Treasury to pay for those unexpected expenses or unexpected shortfalls in tax income. And if there isn't a deficit, there will be a surplus of tax income to help grow the government's treasury account.

But the United States doesn't have a surplus. They have a very substantial deficit. What's worse, there isn't any money in the Treasury for the government to borrow from. This serious deficit situation has forced the government to take on massive amounts of debt to pay the bills.

How big of a number are we talking about? In 2012, the United States deficit was over $1 trillion.

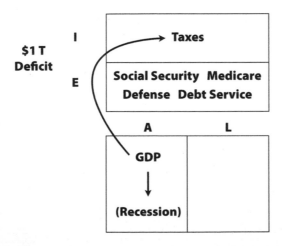

One of the reasons cash flow is so important when conducting a fundamental analysis is that it can tell us, as investors, if an entity is cash-flow positive. Or what I see as being financially *solvent*. As we look at the situation of the United States, we can see that it is cash-flow negative, or what I see as financially *insolvent*. Rich dad would see this as a sign of financial cancer. It is the one number that instantly tells you there might be trouble. This type of simple fundamental analysis helps us gain insight into the financial strength or weakness of an entity. It is possible that a deficit might just be a short-term bump in the road. Most of the time, however, a deficit spells trouble.

The income statement of the United States shows a policy of deficit spending. Congress has actively chosen to continue spending more and more money that it does not have, which means it is forced to take on an ever-growing mountain of debt to pay for this spending. Even a beginning investor can easily see the relationship between the U.S income statement and its fiscal policies.

Seeing into the Future Through Policy and Demographics

Ugly numbers are littered across the financial statement of the United States government. As of this writing, the deficit is now pushing again to more than $1 trillion and there is an *on-balance-sheet debt* of close to $17 trillion. However, that is only the beginning of the problem. The ugliest number that the United States is facing is not on the balance sheet at all. But it will have a massive impact on it in the next few years. It is the impact that demographics will have on current U.S. fiscal policy.

In March of 2011, *Investment Outlook* published an article by William H. Gross of PIMCO titled "Skunked." In his report, he cites that Medicare, Medicaid, and Social Security account for 44 percent of federal spending, and this percentage is rising steadily.

After World War II, the United States experienced a population explosion known as the *baby boom*. Most of these baby boomers are not yet eligible to collect Social Security, Medicare, and Medicaid. But in the coming years they will be, and the policy of the U.S. government is to give these baby boomers what they have been promised. Because these promises are financial commitments that don't yet show up as debt, they are *off-balance-sheet promises.*

Here is an example to help you see how off-balance-sheet promises work. When you borrow money from the bank to purchase a car, this debt is a promise to pay and shows up *on* your balance sheet. You might also have a policy in your household of paying for your children's college education. This policy, however, requires no transaction to be recorded on your balance sheet today. It is an *off-balance-sheet promise.* It is a promise to pay that is every bit as powerful as the promise you made to the bank to pay off the car loan. A promise is a promise. The bank is *entitled* to the money that you've promised to pay. Your children are also *entitled* to the money you promised them. Whether or not it's a good idea to promise your children to pay for things in the future is not relevant. If you begin to look at your future and factor in the rising cost of education, you could be paying a lot of money. But a promise is a promise, and when they reach college age they will expect to collect on that promise—no matter the cost to you. So while your car loan would show up on your balance sheet as a $50,000 liability, the promise to your kids (which the credit agencies would never see) could total over a million dollars. If you have no money available when your kids come to collect on your promise, you will have to borrow it. In some ways you are now running a Ponzi scheme because you are now making new promises you can't keep in an effort to meet old promises. The off-balance-sheet debt will eventually migrate onto the balance sheet. This is what's happening to sovereign balance sheets all over the world today.

Some people think they could get rich as an investor if they only had a crystal ball to tell them the future. The truth is you don't need a crystal ball. Policy plus demographics equals the future. Fundamental analysis today can help you forecast for tomorrow.

The baby boomers in the United States are entitled to having the promises of Social Security, Medicare, and Medicaid fulfilled. If the U.S. government tried to change this policy, the boomers would not be happy.

So let's do a little analysis: If 44 percent of the current federal spending already goes directly to Medicare, Medicaid, and Social Security, what do we imagine will happen when the huge numbers of baby boomers hit retirement age? There are over $100 trillion of entitlement liabilities that will be need to be paid to the baby boomers.

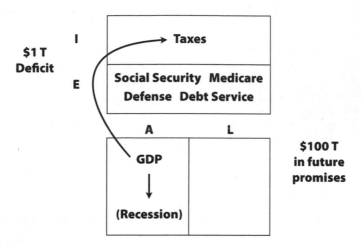

Without thinking (or caring) how their policies might impact the nation's financial statement in the future, politicians promised a lot of people retirement money and coverage for much of their healthcare costs—no matter how expensive it becomes.

Reminder: Fundamental analysis tells you the strength of an entity.

So far we have learned that a basic financial statement gives us the following six numbers.

1. **Income**
2. **Expenses**
3. **Cash Flow**
4. **Assets**
5. **Liabilities**
6. **Equity (net worth)**

For many people it is sometimes easier to draw these numbers as a picture, a common practice at Rich Dad workshops.

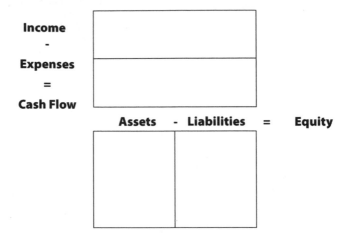

As you get better and better at fundamental analysis you will be able to see relationships between the numbers and get better at judging the strength of entities.

For example, let's look at the relationship of two numbers in our U.S. financial statement: DEBT and GDP as of January 2013:

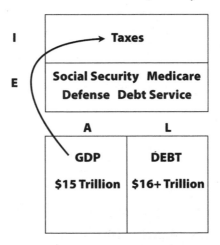

GDP is vital to any country because it is the economic engine that creates cash. The more goods and services a country produces, the more cash the country creates and the more taxes the country can collect. So a country's ability to pay off debt is dependent on its GDP. This can be a very powerful gauge of a country's strength or weakness.

Let's imagine that you are an economist at the prestigious Standard & Poor's financial markets intelligence company. The S&P uses fundamental analysis to determine the financial strength of companies and countries to help investors determine how risky it would be to loan them money. After all, if a country can't pay me back, I might think twice about loaning it my money by purchasing its bonds.

If your job at Standard & Poor's were to give the United States a credit rating, how would you go about it?

You could start by looking at the relationship between its debt and its GDP because it helps you answer the question of whether or not the country has a strong enough GDP to enable it to collect the taxes it needs to pay its debts.

KEY POINT!

DEBT/GDP RATIO
Does this nation have a strong enough GDP that it can collect enough taxes to pay its debt?

To help tell the story of these two numbers we can view this as a ratio.

DEBT
16 Trillion

GDP
15 Trillion

DEBT/GDP RATIO IS 106%

In other words, as of this writing, the debt that is on that balance sheet of the United States is over 100 percent as large as its GDP. Remember that policy is the reason a financial statement looks the way it does. These numbers don't happen by accident.

Putting the Debt/GDP Ratio into Perspective

When the European Union (EU) introduced the Euro, it set a standard of financial strength for each member country. Because debt/GDP reveals so much about a country's financial strength, it set the criteria of a debt/GDP of no more than 60 percent.

Today, many of the countries in the European Union have pushed well above that bar and investors that are proficient in fundamental analysis see the European debt situation as a serious crisis.

Here are some of the numbers...keeping in mind that these number will change over time:

Italy DEBT/GDP = 120 percent

Greece DEBT/GDP = 165 percent

Portugal DEBT/GDP = 107 percent

Ireland DEBT/GDP = 108 percent

EU AVERAGE DEBT/GDP = 82 percent

In fact, you will find that many of the numbers you'll see when doing a sovereign fundamental analysis will be in relation to the GDP. Any discussion of sovereign fundamental analysis would be incomplete without introducing relationships to GDP.

So you don't get the whole story if you look at a country's expenses alone. You need to look at them relative to GDP. It's also incomplete to just examine a country's deficit; we must look at it relative to the GDP. It's incomplete to just examine a country's taxes; must we look at them compared to the GDP.

Keep the Big Picture in Mind

The overriding point of this chapter is not to cover every detail of sovereign fundamental analysis. It's easy to get caught up in the details. Many teachers, myself included, have a tendency to focus in tighter—getting smaller and smaller—as they teach. Whenever I do this with Robert he scolds me and says, "Andy, you're getting small on me." It's a welcome rebuke because I have learned that as a student we cannot learn the small picture (content) until we learn the big picture (context). Water has little value without the pitcher, and the pitcher is of no use to us without the water. You need to start out with an empty pitcher and make sure it's large enough to hold the water we plan to fill it with. If you have no pitcher at all—or your pitcher isn't large enough—the waters spills to the floor and is lost. So be aware that at this point in your education, I'm only introducing you to things like debt/GDP ratio to help you appreciate the power of the larger lesson:

Fundamental analysis really does help us discover the strength of an entity.

Monetary Policy Is Part of Sovereign Fundamental Analysis

In the United States fiscal policy is set by Congress, and monetary policy is set by the Federal Reserve Bank. The history and ownership of the Federal Reserve—and its relationship to our government—is a long and interesting one that we will explore in another book. But please remember that learning about the Federal Reserve and other central banks is a vital part of your financial education.

KEY POINT!

1. Rate
2. Buy Bonds
✓ **GDP**
✓ **Currency Supply**

Monetary Policy

Federal Reserve

To help your understanding for this discussion, here is a short rundown of the Federal Reserve:

- It is not *federal*, because it is not technically a United States government agency.
- It does not hold *reserves* in the sense that we often think of reserves.
- It is most certainly not a *bank* as we understand the term.

From its own publication, this is how the Federal Reserve describes itself:

> *"The Federal Reserve System is considered to be an independent central bank... The Federal Reserve must work within the framework of the overall objectives of economic and financial policy established by the government; therefore, the description of the System as 'independent within the government' is more accurate."*

By stating that it is independent, the Federal Reserve admits it is not a government entity. It is responsible for its own decisions, and not even the President of the United States can tell it what to do. It gets to decide whether or not it's going to buy Treasury bonds, and it gets to decide whether or not to raise or lower the interest rate. While the U.S. Congress claims to have oversight, there is very little the citizens, or Congress, or even the President can do to affect the actions of the Federal Reserve.

The Federal Reserve has powers to decide the monetary policies of the United States. The two powers that we will concentrate on for the purposes of this book are:

1) The power to change the discount rate (aka interest rate)

2) The power to buy bonds and other securities

By lowering interest rates, the Federal Reserve can incentivize borrowing. That in turn can boost the GDP as people make purchases with the borrowed money. The Fed can also buy Treasury bonds. (And although it seems counterintuitive, the Fed has been given the power to do this with money they print out of thin air!) These two powers cause changes to the currency supply.

Analyzing Monetary Policies

Virtually all the economies of the world are intertwined. From sovereign nations to corporations to individuals, nearly every financial statement exists under the umbrella of the United States and its fundamental numbers. The sheer size of the massive U.S. economy has something to do with it, of course. But this intertwining is also the result of something you may never have heard of: the Bretton Woods System.

The Bretton Woods Agreement dates back to 1944 when the industrial nations of the world agreed that since the United States backed its currency with gold at the time, the dollar would become the world's reserve currency. This means that all the commodities we consume— wheat, barley, oats, frozen concentrated orange juice, gold, silver, and even oil—are measured in U.S. dollars.

Why should you care about Bretton Woods? Because if you are investing in stocks, you will be mindful of sovereign fundamental analysis. You need to know what's happening with the different nations of the world. And most importantly, you need to know about the strength or weakness of the dollar at any given time. Due to the Bretton Woods Agreement, the U.S. dollar affects virtually everything on the planet.

The next chapter in the history of U.S. currency began in 1971 when U.S. President Richard Nixon took the U.S. dollar off the gold standard. But even today, the U.S. dollar represents more than 60 percent of the world reserve currency. That's why stock investors worldwide always want to know how the U.S. dollar is currently performing.

Your Future Can Be Bright

With U.S. policies of deficit spending, pressure for higher taxes, printing money (which devalues the dollar), and the policies of Europe, Japan, and China sending similar messages, many people are afraid of what will happen to the global economy in the future and how they will weather the financial storms that will surely come our way. Never fear! Remember that fundamental analysis is a stepping stone that brings you closer to your goal of stock market cash flow.

Remember that cash flow is all about how you position yourself. It has less to do with good or bad news as the world sees things. With the right education, financial storms can quickly become some of the greatest opportunities. This is why your context is so important

A few years ago my wife and I were vacationing in Orlando, Florida with our kids. I got a phone call early in the morning from Robert asking me if I had seen the news. There had been a huge accident on an oil rig in the Gulf of Mexico. As a result, massive amounts of oil were spewing into the water. It created an environmental nightmare, and it was unclear how the problem would be fixed or how long repairs would take. This was terrible news from almost every angle. But it did not have to be bad financial news as well. When you receive bad news, you have two choices: 1) You can cry about it and hope it changes, or 2) You can position yourself to avoid the problems and possibly even profit from them.

KEY POINT!

**It is not about good or bad news.
It is about how you are positioned!**

Robert and I discussed the different ways an investor could reposition himself during such an event. The company responsible for the accident was British Petroleum. The first step was to evaluate the financial strength of that company to see how well they could deal with this crisis.

BUILD ON IT

**PILLAR #3: CASH FLOW
There is no good or bad
news, only position.**

Are you beginning to see how valuable fundamental analysis can be in deciding how to position yourself? There is no question that the sovereign fundamentals in Europe, Asia, and the United States help determine how investors position themselves. And when it comes to individual stocks, fundamentals are there to help you position yourself more intelligently.

Corporate Financial Statements

With that important insight, let's begin looking at how to evaluate stocks that we might want to invest in. To do so, we will show some ways to perform fundamental analysis of the corporations that issue stock to the public. Specifically, we will look at corporate financial statements to calculate value and determine risk that will help us make intelligent decisions on the purchase of stocks.

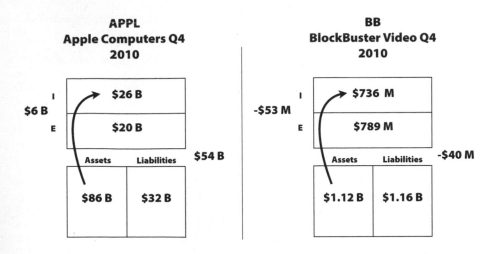

Here are two corporate financial statements. On the left is Apple Computer, developer of the iMac, iPod, iPhone, iTunes, and other popular products. And on the right we have Blockbuster, the company that provided their customers with movie rentals. As you may know, Blockbuster was a video rental company that declared bankruptcy and was then acquired for pennies on the dollar by a satellite broadcasting company. It was a victim of technologic obsolescence. The advent of new technology made Blockbuster's business model obsolete. Who wants to drive over to a video rental place when they can just download the same video at home?

Take a look at the Apple statement first. At the end of 2010, Apple had about $86 billion in assets. Now, it also cost the company some money to make that $86 billion, but generating that income from the assets, Apple made about $26 billion the last quarter of that year. That's a lot of revenue, by any standard. Of course Apple also had expenses. It had to pay employees, rent, fuel, raw materials...all kinds of minuses on the balance sheet. It had assets that produced money, but it spent $20 billion to make those assets possible. Still, it had reported $6 billion profit within a quarter.

Now, another thing Apple did was to take on some debt because it wanted to grow really, really fast. And sure, $6 billion in profit isn't bad, but you could grow a lot faster if you borrowed $32 billion, and Apple did just that. So it had $32 billion in liabilities.

As we learned in the previous chapter, it's always good to look at the relationship between debt and assets. For Apple, the assets were far greater than the liabilities, which put it in a very strong position as compared to what we saw on the U.S. financial statement. In my opinion, the United States is abusing its debt; Apple, on the other hand, is using its debt wisely.

Using debt for growth was a good decision for Apple—and its profits prove it. It was more powerful to leverage the money out of debt than to pay out of earnings. As investors, we need to realize this principle and use it in our evaluations. I don't care if a company like Apple has some debt, as long as it's using the debt to grow and not to pay for liabilities. If it is solvent, then debt is not a problem. In the case of Apple, it was certainly solvent with $6 billion of profits each quarter.

Looking again at the balance sheet, one might wonder why Apple didn't just pay off its debt from its huge asset base. If it did, its asset base would drop to $54 billion. It's much harder to generate $26 billion from that smaller amount of assets. Apple was using some leverage with debt. And it was doing it very well.

The financial statement of Blockbuster tells a different story. It had $1.12 billion in assets, which it used to produce an income of $736 million. But it was very expensive to generate that revenue. From the income statement we can see that its expenses were $786 million, leaving it with a $53 million loss for the quarter. At that time, Blockbuster was not solvent.

The first step toward bankruptcy is *insolvency*, meaning the income is less than expenses. The second step is *default*, which is when an entity can't pay its bills. In the case of Blockbuster, it had debts of $1.16 billion. When we subtract its liabilities from its assets to calculate the equity, we can see that it had a negative equity of $400 million. And with negative cash flow, the situation looked bleak. Blockbuster was in a very difficult situation.

Stock Prices Don't Indicate Investment Quality

It's pretty likely that you've heard the old adage, "You get what you pay for." Well, it's often true when it comes to buying stock.

Some naïve investors focus all their efforts on finding what they think are "affordable" stocks. But the price of a stock is only part of the story. As an investor, you need to always be considering value. Price is what you pay...and value is what you receive.

BUILD ON IT

PILLAR #1: FUNDAMENTALS
A stock's value is based on more than its price.

Let's look at Apple and Blockbuster again. At the end of 2010, Apple shares were trading at more than $300. Some people would say that such prices were far too expensive. They might think that a stock such as Blockbuster was far better because it was available for just six cents per share. They'd be right if they were just looking at price. But fundamental analysis lets us consider value instead.

Looking closely at Apple's financial statement, we see that it had strong cash flow and an excellent debt/assets ratio. Its fundamentals were sound and the stock offered an investor real value, even though the actual stock price appeared to be high. Smart investors responded by buying Apple stock.

Blockbuster's fundamentals were very poor. Despite this, there were uneducated investors who were willing to buy Blockbuster's stock at six cents per share. I can imagine them thinking, "Hey, it's Blockbuster, it's been around for a long time. I can't believe its stock price is so cheap, I need to grab some while it's so low. This thing has got to go up. What have I got to lose?"

Investing is about making smart decisions to grow your money and create positive cash flow. When you make a poor decision, you are undermining that goal. It doesn't matter if the price of a stock is really low or really high—we need to focus on buying value that will help us achieve our investing goals.

Blockbuster has since gone bankrupt, providing us with another valuable investing lesson. People who fish for these penny stocks in hopes of netting a big winner often go home empty-handed. When you buy something with almost zero value, you are hoping against reason that it will pay off. However, this approach isn't investing—it's gambling. And smart investors rarely gamble.

Valuation

With fundamental analysis we have gained some valuable tools to examine an entity and determine its strengths and weaknesses. This leads us to the next logical step: Determining the real value of a stock based on the fundamental numbers. This is a key point called *valuation*.

KEY POINT!	
VALUATION	
How do we determine price?	How do we determine value?
Price = What you pay	Value = What you receive
Changes with SUPPLY and DEMAND	Changes with EARNINGS and GROWTH
Story is told with TECHNICALS	Story is told with FUNDAMENTALS

As you may have noticed, stock prices don't just have a price tag on them like a package of paper towels in the grocery store. They tend to fluctuate all day while the stock market is open. These fluctuations occur because of supply and demand. When investors think the price of a stock makes it a good value, they rapidly buy the stock forcing the price to go up.

When the price gets to a point where investors think it is overvalued, they start selling and force the price down.

As investors, we need to be aware of what we think a stock is worth and what the price of that stock is in the market. To develop this valuation, we consider the company's earnings and growth.

Price/Earnings Ratio—the PE

Earnings represent how much money the company makes. The price investors are willing to pay for a stock is largely based on how much money the company generates. The more money a company earns, the more valuable it is to investors, which means they are generally willing to pay a higher price to own that stock.

As we learn to determine the value of a stock, we'll be in a much better position to make good investment decisions that will help us achieve those goals of growing our money and creating cash flow. To do this, let's look again at the income statement, the balance sheet, and some new relationships between price and the earnings.

One of my goals since becoming a parent has been to provide my sons with experiential learning. I don't worry about home schooling versus public schooling; I do both. When I want to teach my sons about volcanoes, we fly to Hawaii and see a real volcano. When we study space travel, we go to Kennedy Space Center in Florida. They go to public school, and they learn a lot there, but I don't rely on that system alone to teach them everything I want them to learn. (Of course, all this takes money, and we have invested a lot of money tied to these life goals. There's nothing that moves me more deeply than watching my kids learn).

So when I wanted to start teaching my kids about money, I helped them start a business. I didn't want their first income to come from shoveling snow from somebody's walkway or washing windows. I wanted them to experience what it was like to start a business and offer value through that business to as many people as possible. I want them to grow up with running a business being second nature.

My boys started Tanner Brothers Ice Cold Lemonade when they were just little kids—not yet even in first grade. They learned very quickly that people would show up because they were cute. But they would come back if they delivered value. So we spent some time and built a nice wooden lemonade stand that they could take pride in. They spent some time experimenting with different recipes until they found a truly superior lemonade. They found a venture capitalist (me) and an intern for cheap labor (named Mom). They were set.

Let's take a look at their initial financials. They started with an investment of $30. With this capital they went to the store and spent $20 on ice, lemons, and sugar. This represents their expenses. On a hot Saturday morning they opened up the stand and immediately made $50. So here's how their business looked in numbers:

Revenue = $50

Expenses = $20

Earnings = $30

EXPENSES: lemons, sugar, water, cups = $20
REVENUE: sales, tips = $50

Revenue = $50
Expenses = $20
_____
Earnings = $30

They now easily make more than that $30 every time they set up the stand. They post a schedule on Facebook (https://www.facebook.com/tannerbroslemonade#) so people know when they're open for business and they find a line waiting for them when they open. They have built a reputation for value that exceeds their cuteness (and let me tell you, they're pretty cute) and that has increased the value of their business.

With a little taste of business success, let's say my boys decide they want to grow it even more. They might make the decision to raise more capital by selling one hundred shares in the company to investors.

Based on their experience, they believe they can generate a minimum of $30 of income every Saturday. Divided into 100 shares, we can see that each share represents 30 cents. This is what we call *earnings per share*.

	EARNINGS	EARNINGS PER SHARE
Tanner Bros.	**$30**	
		That's 30¢ in
	SHARES	**earnings for every**
Ice Cold Lemonade	**100**	**share**

At this point, let's suppose you walk past this lemonade stand and you reckon you would like a share of the business. How much should you pay for that share? You look at the earnings and see that if you buy one share you will make 30 cents every Saturday. Think of the lemonade stand as simply a machine that can generate 30 cents for you each Saturday without having to do any of the work! When you go to buy the shares you will be competing against other investors, and there are only 100 shares of stock being offered to the public. Thus the price of the shares will be determined by supply and demand.

When the shares become available to the public, you see the share price settles in at $3 per share.

So how can you know if $3 per share is a good deal for you?

One place to start is comparing this opportunity to others that are being offered in the neighborhood. If you can see what other investors are willing to pay for the earnings of other companies, you can get an idea of the relative value of this lemonade stand. Let's say you know that there are two other businesses in the neighborhood with shares available where you could invest your money.

The Smith brothers have a lawn mowing business, and the Jones brothers wash windows.

The Smith Brothers shares have a share price of $2.50.

The Jones Brothers have a share price of $2.00.

Most people would think that the Jones brothers have a better value because their stock is less expensive per share. But you should not look at shares of a stock the same way you shop for things at a store. In the stock market, price simply tells us what we have to pay to own the stock. Price does not tell us anything about what we receive. To better gauge the value, we need to look at the earnings.

How much are investors willing to pay to own a share of each business?

25¢ earnings per share

Share price is $2.50

20¢ earnings per share

Share price is $2.00

You can see the Smith Brothers have a higher share price, but they also deliver greater earnings per share. The Jones bothers have the cheaper stock, but their company produces a smaller amount of earnings for each share.

KEY POINT!

PRICE EARNINGS RATIO

How much are investors willing to pay for $1 of earnings?

Price = What you pay   Earnings = What you receive

If you look closely you will discover that investors in both companies are actually receiving the same amount of value when it comes to earnings.

In the case of the Smith brothers, investors are paying $2.50 per share to get 25¢ of earnings. That means that to get $1 of earnings they are paying $10.

In the case of the Jones brothers, investors are paying $2.00 per share to get 20¢ of earnings. That means to get $1 of earnings; investors in both companies are paying $10.

With an understanding of P/E ratios, you have a huge insight into how much to bid to own shares of the lemonade stand. You know there are opportunities in the neighborhood to get a dollar of earnings for about $10. You know that if you pay more than $10 dollars for $1 of earnings for a business in this neighborhood, you will have to find what factors, if any, justify the price.

How much are investors willing to pay to own a share of each business?

Now when we look at Tanner Brothers at $3 per share it makes more sense.

By looking at the other businesses and seeing what investors are willing to pay for one dollar of earnings, the Tanner Brothers can get a sense of what their business is worth. For Tanner Brothers, the price is $3, and the earning per each share is 30¢. All three businesses have P/E ratios of 10.

How much are investors willing to pay to own a share of each business?

You will find that when it comes to earnings, a lower P/E ratio means more bang for the buck. In the real world, though, do people really pay for high P/E ratios? If they feel the company has potential, then they absolutely pay for a high P/E ratio.

Price/Earnings and Growth (PEG)

During the dot-com boom you could find people willing to buy stocks with a P/E ratio of 200 or more—meaning they were paying $200 for $1 of earnings. There were actual cases of P/Es that were undefined because the company had not yet made any earnings. Were these investors nuts? Why would investors do this? The answer is future growth.

There was a day, in the early stages of every company, when the company had no earnings. In the 1990s many investors got so caught up in the new startup company frenzy of the dot-com boom, they did not pay much attention to earnings. They saw value in growth, and they were willing to pay for it. We can learn many lessons from the greed of the dot-com bubble.

In the diagram below it is not hard to see that in the context of earnings, company ABC is bringing more value to its investors today.

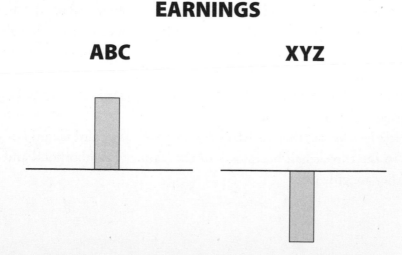

EARNINGS

ABC   **XYZ**

But the stock market is a forward-thinking place. Investors are buying for tomorrow, not for today. If you look at the same two companies in the context of growth, you might have a change of heart as to which one you want to own.

EARNINGS GROWTH

ABC   XYZ

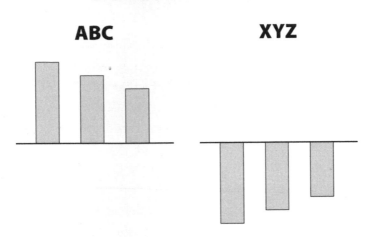

Company ABC is generating earnings today. Company XYZ is losing money today. The inexperienced investor is only looking at the snapshot. We want to look at the trend to determine where future earnings are headed.

Company XYZ's trend tells me something about value. If I buy a stock, I'm paying for earnings because that is part of value. But what about growth? Is a company that is growing more valuable than a company that's not? How can we measure growth as a part of value?

The price I pay for the stock is one factor. The earnings I receive for my investment is another factor.

Now let's look at the growth of the company as a third factor. Let's go back to the three small businesses in the Tanner neighborhood and see how they are growing.

How much are investors willing to pay to own a share of each business?

When we looked at the price investors paid for earnings, we saw that each business was giving investors the same value for the earnings. But growth is a different story. When investors buy shares of Tanner Brothers, they are getting a company that is growing at 20 percent. Moreover, analysts are projecting that it will have similar growth next year. If it earns even more next year, investors will be getting even more bang for their buck, and it is likely that the share price will rise.

You can see why investors would be willing to pay for earnings, and also why they would be willing to pay for growth.

KEY POINT!
PRICE EARNINGS RATIO
How much are investors willing to pay for $1 of earnings?
Price = What you pay   Earnings = What you receive

PEG ratio gives us information on three variables: the price of the shares, the earnings of the company, and the growth of the company earnings.

How about growth?

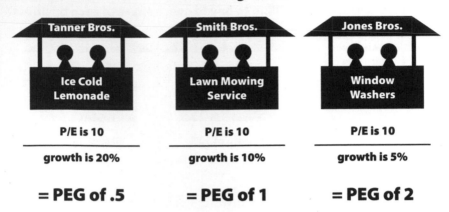

Tanner Brothers has a very low PEG ratio. That tells you as an investor that for the price you are paying, you are going to get more value for your buck.

It's always important to keep the big picture in mind.

In our discussion on sovereign fundamentals we found that using ratios helped us understand the relationship between two numbers. I'm terrible at math, and I really don't care to do a lot of calculations. I don't like fractions and numerators and denominators and all that stuff. I just want to learn to tell the story of the financial statement.

We learned in our discussions on sovereign fundamentals that ratios often include the relationship between GDP and some other number in the financial statement. When it comes to corporate fundamental analysis, we often encounter ratios that describe the relationship of price to some other number. Why? Because price is merely what we pay, and we want to figure out what we are getting for our money. When we compare the price to different parts of the financial statement, we can begin to understand what we are actually paying for. That's the big picture we're looking for.

KEY POINT!	
Price ratios help us understand what we are paying for	
Price/Earnings:	**Tells you how much you are paying for EARNINGS**
Price/Book	**Tells you how much you are paying for EQUITY**
Price/Sales	**Tells you how much you are paying for REVENUE**
(Price/Earnings)/ Growth	**Tells you how much you are paying for EARNINGS and GROWTH**

Ratios simply tell us how much money we are spending in relation to how the company is performing in different areas of its financial statement.

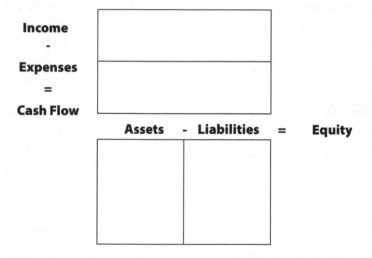

As a *share*holder you want to know how much you are paying for a *share* of the earnings. How much are you paying for a share of the sales? And how much are you paying for a share of the equity? The price by itself really does not mean much. Only when we compare it to the financial statements does it help us understand what kind of value we receive.

How Do You Apply This in the Real World?

Some time ago, Apple Computer hit a new high for the year. Robert called me that day and we talked about Apple's meteoric rise. At first it seemed unlikely that the price would go any higher. The stock chart looked like the price was almost going straight up. Many people were wondering if this was sustainable. Perhaps it was time to change positions and short the stock to make money on a downfall. (We will learn in a later chapter how to short a stock as a way to make money when a stock runs out of gas and goes down).

Remember that price really does not mean much when viewed by itself—even at $400 or $500 a share. In fact, Apple's earnings were actually keeping pace with its stock price. Apple had a P/E ratio around 13 that day. That meant investors were spending about $13 in price for every one dollar of earnings. The average P/E for the average stock in the NASDAQ was around $17. That means the average stock in the NASDAQ was costing investors around $17 in price for every one dollar of earnings. From an earnings standpoint, Apple was still cheap, even though it was at $500 per share!

Apple continued its rise—to $700 a share! Only when the fundamentals began to show a slowdown in their rate of growth did the stock begin to fall. The people who paid attention to price alone should have looked at the fundamentals. Later on we will also see how the second pillar, technical analysis, is also a factor to consider.

Market Capitalization

What if you decided to buy all the shares in a company such as Oracle or Exxon Mobil? As you can imagine, these companies have issued millions and millions of shares of stock. And it would cost you billions of dollars to buy every single share. While coming up with that kind of cash might be very difficult, figuring out the total price tag is very easy. This is known as *market capitalization*, or *market cap* for short. Simply do a little research to discover how many shares are currently issued, and then find the current price of those shares.

If we go back to our smaller lemonade-stand example, a total buyout might be within your budget:

Market Capitalization

100 shares

$3 per share

Market Cap is $300

You can see that market capitalization is a number we can easily calculate to determine the value of an entire company. For the Tanner Brothers lemonade business, we multiply the share price of $3 by the number of outstanding shares (100) to get the market capitalization of $300.

**Market Capitalization = (Share Price)
x (Number of Outstanding Shares)**

The market cap is the price you'd have to pay to buy every share and own an entire company.

At the other end of the spectrum, Apple has a very high market capitalization—in the hundreds of billions, making it among the largest companies in America. With a wide variety of companies—all with different amounts of market capitalization—investors categorize companies according to their market caps:

Market Capitalization

Small Cap
$300 million to $2 billion
(supposedly likely to have more growth potential)

Mid Cap
$2 Billion to $10 billion
(likely more growth potential)

Large Cap
Greater that $10 Billion
(supposedly more likely to be well established)

Risk **Growth**

But is one type of market capitalization better than another?

The thinking here is that the large cap companies are well-established, their balance sheets are big, and there is, at least in theory, less risk. The smaller companies have more room for growth; potentially they could go big-time. But with small-caps there's more risk; they may never make it. A small-cap company could blow up, but it could also blow out. It could do well or it could do poorly. To try to work out a most likely scenario, you need to know something about its earnings, the stock price, the number of shares, its market capitalization, and if it's showing signs of growth.

Some Valuable Investing Vocabulary

Part of what we're trying to do here is to learn the vocabulary that helps us to translate information into meaning. If you don't have this vocabulary when you watch the financial news, read a periodical, talk with your advisors, or go to buy a stock, then the information may have less meaning for you. Each asset class—business, real estate, stocks, commodities—has its own vocabulary.

This chapter is adding several new words to your investing vocabulary: PE, PEG, market capitalization, etc. Understanding these words makes you a more intelligent investor and helps you progress along the Education Continuum™.

Now let's do a wealth-building activity to put some meaning to these numbers and vocabulary.

Education Activity

In Chapter One I challenged you to do more than just read this book. I challenged you to discuss what you are reading with others and to find activities to enhance your learning. You can practice everything we've discussed so far by comparing several different stocks—their values, their PEs, their PEGs. You can do this if you have some stocks of your own or you can do it by choosing some stocks at random. If you don't have a current software service you prefer, you can easily use a free service such as *Yahoo! Finance* or *Google Finance* to get this information.

Education Activity

Market Cap	
Enterprise value	
Trailing P/E	
Forward P/E	
PEG Ratio	
Price/Sales	
Price/Book	

Revenue
-
Expenses
=
Earnings

Assets - Liabilities = Equity

This can be a lot like a game or a treasure hunt. Try to find the information for each valuation in the table. Also try to visualize what part of the financial statement the valuation is related to. When you focus on an individual stock, look for the *key statistics* (that's an actual category on some websites such as *Yahoo! Finance*) to view all the essential information.

First we have market cap, or **market capitalization**. We now know this is the total dollar value of the company. Choose a company and see if you can find information on its market cap.

Enterprise value is similar to the market cap, but it includes the liabilities. So it tells us that if we actually owned the stock, we'd have some cash and some debt to deal with.

The *P/E* is the *price/earnings ratio*. The **trailing P/E** is this ratio as of yesterday. And ***ttm*** stands for *trailing twelve months*, meaning (as you've probably guessed) that the numbers are measuring at the earnings over the last 12 months and are the ratio between those earnings and the *intraday* price (average price over the course of the current day).

With the *forward P/E*, you can project what the **fiscal year** ahead might look like. But that's not necessarily a reason to hold off buying the stock, because the price could be more expensive then.

Look at the *PEG ratio* expected for the next five years. A PEG of 0.5 or better means that the company is growing really well. A PEG of two or more means it is not growing as well.

What's our next statistic? **Price/sales**. This is simply the share price divided by the sales revenue. It's the relationship between the cost of the share and the income generated by sales. This is not earnings, because we have not yet subtracted the expenses. It doesn't represent the company's profit or loss—just the sales. The *price/sales ratio* tells you how much every dollar you have paid for the stock is generating in sales.

How about *price/book*? This ratio gives us the accounting value of the equity. This is what you are paying for your assets in the most recent quarter (MRQ).

We don't need to be too concerned, right now, with the next two ratios...but here are the definitions. *Enterprise value/revenue* simply gives a measure of the value of the company in relation to its revenues. And *enterprise value/EBITDA* is a measure of the value of the company in relation to its earnings before interest, tax, depreciation, and amortization (EBITDA).

You can look at any stock in this way, learning a bit about value, fundamental analysis, and the strength of an entity.

Next, see how your stocks compare to each other.

Stock comparison

Proctor & Gamble Co. Jul 8, 2012	
Market Cap (intraday)	167.91B
Enterprise Value (Jul 8, 2012)	198.41B
Trailing P/E (ttm, intraday)	18.79
Forward P/E (fye Jun 30, 2013)	15.67
PEG Ratio (5 yr expected)	2.45
Price/Sales (ttm)	1.97
Price/Book (mrq)	2.62
Share price (Jul 8, 2012)	$61.28

Apple Inc. Jul 8, 2012	
Market Cap (intraday)	566.54B
Enterprise Value (Jul 8, 2012)	538.00B
Trailing P/E (ttm, intraday)	14.76
Forward P/E (fye Sep 24, 2013)	11.18
PEG Ratio (5 yr expected)	0.6
Price/Sales (ttm)	4.01
Price/Book (mrq)	5.56
Share price (Jul 8, 2012)	$605.88

Let's compare Proctor & Gamble (P&G) and Apple. Both are large-cap companies with market capitalization of more than $10 billion. But there's a big difference in the price of Apple shares, when it was trading at around $600, and the price of P&G, trading around $60

Proctor & Gamble Co. Jul 8, 2012	
Trailing P/E (ttm, intraday)	18.79
PEG Ratio (5 yr expected)	2.45

Apple Inc. Jul 8, 2012	
Trailing P/E (ttm, intraday)	14.76
PEG Ratio (5 yr expected)	0.6

Even at 10 times the price, Apple gives the investor more earnings for the price. Based on this analysis, it also looks like Apple gives more value in terms of growth than P&G. So why would anyone choose P&G?

Traditionally P&G has had a policy of paying a dividend of about 3.7 percent. Apple has only recently begun to pay dividends, but has not paid them in the past.

So while a person might want to know which stock is better than the other, the answer is that it depends on that individual's personal goals. If your goal is for income, you might adopt a policy of buying stocks that pay a high dividend. Therefore, you might be willing to pay a little more in P/E if you can actually get a return on your money in the form of a dividend.

Don't forget about that dreaded obsolescence risk. In this example, P&G offers less of it, meaning its products are less likely to become outdated with new advancements in technology.

Other investors are more interested in growth. In that case, a stock such as Apple may be more appealing. Apple reinvests a large amount of its earnings into growing the company and developing new technology to fight obsolescence risk. Because of that, it might have less money to pay in dividends. But the share price is likely to go higher—if the company does grow.

As we have seen, Apple and P&G are two very different types of stocks for investors. Depending upon your own financial goals, you could be interested in one or the other of these stocks to help you achieve what you are looking for—income or growth—to improve your personal financial statement.

Now let's look at Apple and compare it to other stocks in the same technology sector.

Technology Sector Jul 2012		Apple Inc. Jul 2012	
Trailing P/E (ttm, intraday)	17.35	Trailing P/E (ttm, intraday)	14.76

Apple's P/E came in lower than the average P/E for the technology sector. So while some people might feel uncomfortable spending hundreds of dollars per share, they can take comfort in knowing that they are still getting more bang for their buck than with the average tech stock.

Personal Fundamental Analysis

At the beginning of this chapter, I said that fundamental analysis could give us answers about the financial strength of any entity.

Personal

Corporate

Sovereign

Now that we have explored fundamental analysis of sovereign nations and corporations, let's turn our attention inward. As we analyze our own personal financial statements using these same tools and numbers, we can begin to see our true financial health. Knowing this information can help us address our own policies in achieving our financial goals.

This is also a good point to remind ourselves about the relationship between financial statements and policy.

KEY POINT!

Why does a financial statement look the way it does? POLICY!

While we cannot change government policy or corporate policy all by ourselves, we can change our personal policies. This is good news. You control your own destiny. No matter how poorly the world economy becomes, if your own personal financial statement is healthy, you will be safe. When it comes to your own personal financial statement, you can be in total control.

> **KEY POINT!**
>
> **If you don't like how your financial statement looks, then change your policies**

Lessons from Real Estate

To begin our discussion of personal fundamental analysis, let's start with an investing analogy related to real estate. As investors, there are three ways we can use real estate to accomplish our goals:

- Capital gain: buy a new house and then flip it to earn a capital gain on our money

- Cash flow: buy a new house and rent it to earn income for ongoing cash flow

- Hedge: buy insurance on the property to protect it

All three of these are valid actions. And we can also achieve all of them in any asset class. One is not better than another, because it all depends on our own individual investing goals. It's important that we know about these different options so we can make smart decisions.

As a reminder, let's see how these different investment approaches appear on our financial statements. When you buy a house in hopes that the value of it will grow to achieve a capital gain, you will enter the value of that house in your asset column. At that point, the value of that investment can grow or decrease in value, depending on the market. This fluctuation will affect your net worth. Knowing this, you can ask yourself this important question: "What are my investing goals? Is one of them to increase my net worth? If so, what investments should I buy to accomplish this?" Stock investors have a similar option available to them. If they want to increase their net worth with stocks, they can buy shares and hold them in their portfolio, hoping they increase in value. Many people are already doing this through retirement plans such as 401(k)s, IRAs, and mutual funds.

However, if you decide to rent that house to someone else you will generate cash flow from your asset. Cash flow is valuable to you because it's how you are able to feed your family and pay your bills. Simply having an asset that increases your net worth does nothing to improve your cash flow situation. That's why Robert encourages people around the world to think differently and seek to buy assets that give them cash flow. When we have assets that generate cash flow for us, it can help us now and through retirement. Remember: Net worth doesn't help you retire; cash flow does. That's an important distinction to make. If you are renting your houses, that is cash flow that goes into your income statement. It's an important addition to your income statement that can transform your life.

Our third investing option is *hedging*. In the real estate world it is known as insurance. You put a hedge into your liability column because it doesn't increase your net worth or provide you with income. It is simply a purchase that protects you if something bad happens to your primary investment.

In Robert's book, *Unfair Advantage: The Power of Financial Education*, he asked me about the biggest difference between professional and amateur investors. I said that amateurs are always going for the capital gain, and professionals go for cash flow. Amateurs are always trying to hedge or protect themselves with diversification, but professionals use contracts like insurance.

Capital Gain or Cash Flow?

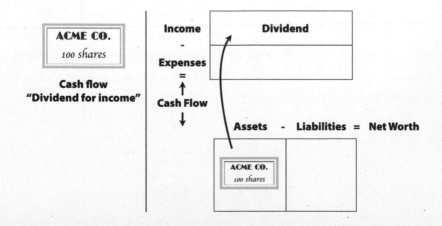

That simple example with real estate applies to stocks in the same way. Maybe you want to buy Acme...and you buy it at $100 a share. And maybe you sell it at $200. Now your net worth's gone up. You have more money than you did before. Your assets have grown, but Acme has not given you any income; there's no cash flow from it.

But suppose you buy a stock that pays you a regular dividend. Now you own an asset that is also adding to your cash flow without you having to do a thing for it. With enough assets like this, you can eventually have the income to do whatever you like—right now or in retirement. In my opinion, that should be the overall goal of investing: freedom of choice and lifestyle.

Today's typical retirement plans, such as the 401(k), don't provide us with cash flow. Instead, the focus is usually trying to build a net worth that is large enough to support retirement—and that is very hard to do. Many people are concerned that their money will run out before their time on earth does.

Many mutual funds are not created to provide us with cash flow. Instead, they simply add—or sometimes subtract—from our net worth. But they are not giving us income.

For some new investors, this is a difficult concept to understand. We are trained by the media and Wall Street to equate net worth growth with investing success. But let's look at a familiar situation that illustrates why net worth may not be the best investing goal.

Suppose you have $4,000 each month in your expense column. You've got a $4,000 nut to crack each month. Well, having your net worth go up and down isn't really going to matter. You need to cover these expenses every month. You need income-producing assets to produce cash that helps crack this nut. If you can get $4,000 in cash flow coming from assets, you can be independent of a job. Now, that's a goal!

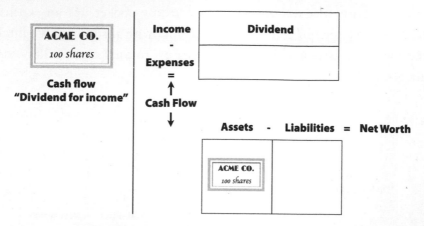

That is wealth. Wealth is when you have passive income to crack that $4,000 nut, rather than making $4,000 of active income from a job each month.

I believe the key to wealth is cash flow. If someone has a high net worth, he or she may be rich but may still have to work. You can be rich in net worth and not be able to pay your bills. You can have a million dollars in a 401K and not be able to crack your monthly-expenses nut for the rest of your life. But with passive income that exceeds expenses, then you've become independently wealthy. In other words, you have enough wealth to be independent from having to work.

Hedging

Now let's take a quick look at hedging, which is essentially buying insurance on investments. When I buy an investment such as a house, I certainly don't want to lose that investment. No matter the reason behind my purchase, it's important to protect it. If the house burns down, the insurance I have bought guarantees that my investment will be safe. If I bought the house to live in, the insurance will pay for a new one to be built. If I bought it for capital gains, then the structure will be restored so I can sell it in the future. And if I bought it for cash flow, I can get renters back into it fairly quickly.

Buying insurance doesn't put money in my pocket. It's an expense. But smart investors protect their investments with insurance. We'll talk more about this later in this book when we get to the Fourth Pillar—risk management.

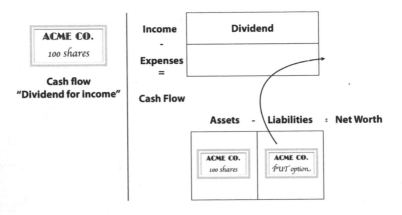

The Personal Financial Statement

All these lessons we have been learning are especially applicable to the most important fundamental analysis of all—your own personal financial statement. This is why so many investors still walk with a spring in their step when the data on the corporate level, and especially the sovereign level, looks grim. Unlike looking at fundamentals on the corporate and sovereign levels, you get to make polices for yourself, at the personal level. Many people like to complain about the government policies of their country or the corporate policies of a company. But you rarely see folks evaluating their personal financial policies. This is a perfect time to once again remind ourselves of a key point we introduced early in the chapter:

KEY POINT!

Why does a financial statement look the way it does? POLICY!

Why does the U.S. financial statement look so bad? Fiscal and monetary policy. Why does a company financial statement look so good at the same moment? Corporate policy. So why does your financial statement look the way it does? You guessed it: personal financial policy.

If you want to change or improve your financial statement, then change your policy. For example, when it comes to income, you can choose a policy of working for money or a policy of having money work for you. When it comes to financial education, you can choose a policy of ignorance and hoping for the best, or a policy of education and actively seeking the best. In fact, as you look at the numbers in your financial statement, each number has a lot to do with your personal financial policies. Ask yourself what your policy is on the part of the financial statement. For example, when it comes to income, is your policy to work for money or have money work for you? Most often an upgrade in lifestyle requires an increase in expenses. Is your policy to cover expense increases by acquiring assets or hoping for a raise? Examine each of the following elements of your financial statement and reflect on your policy for each one.

- **Income**
- **Expenses**
- **Cash Flow** (income minus expenses)
- **Assets**
- **Liabilities**
- **Equity or net worth** (assets minus liabilities)
- **Credit score**
- **Buying power**

Buying Power and Education

There are really only two constraints on any of us when it comes to getting rich:

1. Do we have the ability to intelligently recognize a solid asset?

2. Do we have the resources to seize opportunity?

In other words, it really comes down to smarts and buying power. Without either of those two things, we could be facing other investing tragedies:

"I could have bought some Google shares when the company
first went public—had I only known!"

or

"I knew that gold was likely to double in value,
but I had no money to buy it"

KEY POINT!

Two limiting factors to buying assets:

1. We want the education we need to know a good deal from a bad deal

2. We want the buying power to seize the opportunity

What is your buying power number? In other words, how large of an asset could you buy today? Ken McElroy might be the best Rich Dad Advisor to demonstrate this. If Kenny's buying power were limited to his savings account, he might miss out on many opportunities. So he has built tremendous relationships with other investors and banks to harness buying power. He is a master at raising capital and is never constrained by using his own money. Pause for a moment and reflect on the following statement:

The rich invest as if they have no money.

In fact the ultimate goal for the super-wealthy is to never invest with their own money. They are masters of leverage and raising capital.

If Robert or Ken lost everything they had, I'm confident they would be back on top very quickly because how they invest would not change.

When you do a fundamental analysis on your personal financial statement, be specific about your buying power and seek to grow that number in cash, credit, relationships, or other forms of funding. What is your policy when it comes to buying power? Cutting up you credit cards decreases your buying power. Or is your policy to use credit wisely? Kim Kiyosaki used a credit card for the down payment on her first rental property—a property that generated cash flow from day one.

As you look at your own situation, it's common to ask yourself this question:

Which of these numbers should I improve?

Are you operating at a deficit? Is your net worth negative? Is your income dependent upon a job? Are you making payments for mortgages, loans, and taxes? Is your credit poor? For some, the decision will be to overcome a deficit and become cash-flow-positive. Others may want to increase their buying power and education. And there are many other strategies that an investor could address. **These decisions become your policies.**

If we look at a financial statement that is weak and want to improve it, what part of the financial statement should we work on? Almost invariably, people believe that if they earn more money their problems will be solved. "If I only made more money, I would be better off," is something we frequently hear.

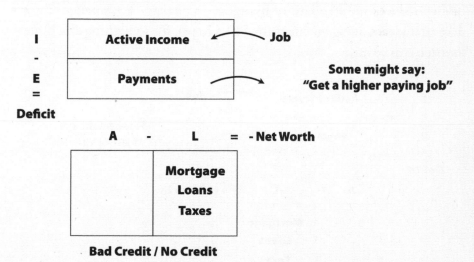

The two most common ways of getting more money boil down to "Get a job" and "Live small." These are policies.

If you want more money, get a job. That's a common way of thinking. Get a job, get a second job, work harder, work longer, and increase your active income. In any case, your expenses are going to remain the same. If your policy is to pay those expenses by getting a job, or a second job, then you are always going to need that job, and that second job. If I'm going to work at a job as my source of income, I'm always going to have to have a job to make my payments on food, clothing, health, and shelter. I don't see how getting a job helps the long-term issue of expenses.

The other common way of thinking I see is living small. "Act your wage," I've heard it said. Cut expenses, clip coupons, buy less, lower your standard of living. This idea is not creative nor illuminating. It requires no financial education, only discipline. Well, I don't like that idea, because now I have to live under the standard of my job, which means my job will dictate my lifestyle and I can never improve upon it. Everything I do in my life will now be under that umbrella and the limitation of a job. If my job is not an abundant thing, then I can't have abundance in my life. And I have to do things like clipping coupons, and going without. That policy reduces my standard of living. It's a goal to 'live smaller.' I don't like that idea. Giving up one thing I like to pay for something else I like is nonsensical to me.

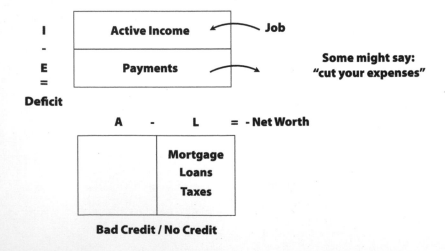

You must decide who you are and what side of the CASHFLOW quadrant will guide your personal financial policies.

Employee

Self Employed

Business Owner

Investor

Clipping coupons and cutting up your credit cards? That's not what investing is about.

As investors, our goal is to generate a passive income stream that is greater than our expenses and to grow our cash flow.

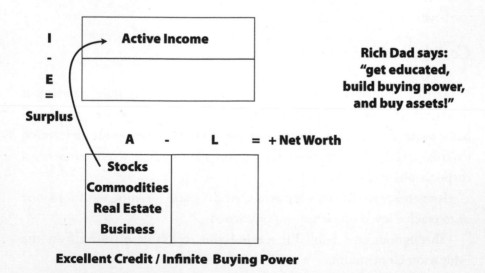

**Rich Dad says:
"get educated,
build buying power,
and buy assets!"**

To achieve these higher goals, you will adopt policies that are often completely the opposite of what you were taught by your parents and your teachers in school. Our policy should be to increase our *buying power*, not reduce it. Our policy would be to quit a job and improve our investing education. That is a sharp contrast to the gurus who say to cut up your credit cards!

KEY POINT!	
Polices are as opposite as the left and right sides of the cash-flow quadrant!	
Policy of financial ignorance: Other people manage my money	Policy of financial education: I am responsible for my money
Policy of lowering buying power: I'm going to cut up my credit cards	Policy of increasing buying power: I'm going develop more relationships with banks and other sources
Policy of active income: 'I want a job'	Policy of passive income: 'I want assets'
Policy of reducing expenses: I'll lower expenses and lower my lifestyle. I'm going to spend less on lattes. I'll save on tax expenses by earning less when I'm old	Policy of increasing expenses: I'll raise my expenses and my lifestyle. I'm going to spend more on assets. I plan on earning and spending more in old age because of inflation.

Conclusion

In this chapter, you started to develop a foundational understanding of fundamentals. Now you understand that virtually any type of organization has a balance sheet and income statement you can analyze to determine its financial health. As you invest, you can analyze a government, a corporation, or even yourself.

Remember to discuss what you're reading and learning with someone or to teach a loved one what you've learned.

Throughout this book I'll remind you to evaluate yourself on the Education Continuum.

The Education Continuum™

Ignorance → Awareness → Competency → Proficiency

When it comes to fundamental analysis, have you become more aware of what is possible? Are you now more competent with some of these skills and strategies? Do you feel a desire to seek out mentors and other education sources to become proficient?

In the next chapter we will be looking at the second pillar of investing: technical analysis. This will give you additional skills and insights you can use.

Remember: the ultimate goal is to gain this knowledge so you can move along the Education Continuum in your quest to become a proficient investor. Rome wasn't built in a day, and neither is your wealth. Take the time to learn these foundational skills and you'll be well on your way to creating your own investing income.

Chapter Summary

Let's review some of the important points of Chapter Four:

1. Investors can do fundamental analysis on three kinds of entities: sovereign, corporate, and personal.

   When we look at the financial statements of any of the three entity types, we can get a sense of the strength of the entity and its value.

2. The financial statement looks the way it does because of policy.

   Certainly, natural disasters such as earthquakes and tsunamis, or political factors such as terrorist attacks, can have an impact on some economies. However, you will generally find that the reason the financial statement looks the way it does is because of the policies made by the leadership of the organization—whether it's a nation, or a company, or a household.

3. Sovereign fundamentals are affected by fiscal policy and monetary policy.

   When we look at the numbers on a financial statement—income, expenses, debt, and deficits—these numbers are usually determined by fiscal policy such as taxation and spending. Central banks such as the Federal Reserve or the European Central Bank dictate monetary policy. As they manipulate currency supply they attempt to have an impact on the country's economy or gross domestic product.

4. Policy plus demographics equals the future.

   As we seek to see what might happen in the future, we don't really need a crystal ball. Because when we apply the policies of the country—or even a corporation—to a certain demographic, the future becomes more clear and complete with dates and deadlines.

5. One of the most important numbers in sovereign fundamental analysis is the debt/GDP ratio.

   This one simple number gives us huge insight into the financial strength or weakness of any country.

6. Good or bad news is less important than how you are positioned.

   Some people become fearful or angry when they look at nations or corporations that are floundering on the brink of disaster. True investors are more concerned with how they are positioned and how their personal financial statement will be affected. The truth is that within every tragedy there is an opportunity for those who are financially educated and prepared to benefit.

7. Corporate fundamental analysis helps us with valuation.

   Price by itself in the stock market really doesn't mean very much. That's because price alone does not reflect the value we will receive. By conducting a corporate fundamental analysis, we can have a much clearer picture of a company.

8. The important numbers that incorporate fundamental analysis are the P/E ratio and the PEG ratio.

   These numbers bring better meaning to the price of the stock because we can see what kind of earnings and growth the company is giving us for our money. It also helps us make comparisons to others in the market to see if we feel comfortable with what we are receiving.

9. If you don't like how the fundamentals look, then change the policy.

   Countries in dire financial straits (such as Greece) have gotten there because of poor fiscal policy and monetary policy. Countries on the verge of financial catastrophe (such as the United States) will only avoid certain collapse by major and drastic changes in their policy. The same is true for corporate policy. Meg Whitman, who became the CEO of Hewlett-Packard, conducted a fundamental analysis on the company and determined that she needed to eliminate 27,000 jobs. That's changing corporate policy.

But the most important policy is your personal financial policy, and it's the one you can control. If you want to change your personal fundamentals, then change your personal financial policies.

10. The two limiting factors for buying assets are education and buying power.

    In order to put an asset in your asset column, you'll need to determine if the asset is a good deal among the many bad deals you will encounter. Also, you will need to have the financial resources to seize the opportunity.

11. Your new policies might be the opposite of what your parents taught you in school or what today's financial gurus start saying.

Chapter Five

Pillar 2: Technical Analysis

With fundamental analysis we looked at numbers from the financial statement to determine financial health. Technical analysis requires that we learn how to read charts to see the story they tell.

Fundamental analysis tells us the strength of an entity. Technical analysis tells us the strength of the market. The stock market goes up based on supply and demand. The real estate market goes up based on supply and demand; the price of anything goes up based on supply and demand.

BUILD ON IT

PILLAR #2: TECHNICALS
Technical analysis tells us the strength of the market.

At its core, you are going to be studying feelings. How do you feel about stocks, how do you feel about this house, how do you feel about technology? If you like it, you'll buy it. Technical analysis studies what people want: supply and demand.

A stock chart does not tell me very much about the company. It doesn't tell me what the company makes. It doesn't tell me what the company does. It doesn't tell me whether it's profitable or not. It doesn't tell me whether it is growing or shrinking. It simply tells you what the price is and has been. That is just supply and demand. It's a history of how people have felt about the price in the past and how they feel about it today.

In this chapter on technical analysis, you will discover:

- How to read a chart, starting with some of the most basic elements, some of the more introductory concerns when people start chart-reading

- How to analyze the behavior of some sample stocks from the charts to apply what you have learned to your own stocks

- How to use the computer, leveraging the technology to look for and identify signals

- The vocabulary used in chart reading and technical analysis

- Various technical tools used in stock analysis

- Some of the criteria used in trading stocks

As you'll recall from the previous chapters, one of the things we learned is that we cannot control the fundamentals of a sovereign nation or a corporation. The same is true of technicals. However, as you will see, we can use technical analysis to choose our cash flow strategy and to manage our risk.

Why We Need to Know Both Fundamental and Technical Analysis

Several years ago there was a story in *BusinessWeek* about the transition at Enron when CEO Jeffrey Skilling resigned and incoming CEO Ken Lay took over. When a CEO of a corporation resigns, the news might trigger a change in the stock price. This was especially true in the case of Enron because investors suspected something fishy might be happening. Here's what *BusinessWeek* had to say about the situation when they interviewed Ken Lay:

> *There's been some concern among investors that perhaps there's more to his resignation than meets the eye. Perhaps accounting or other issues that have not yet come to light. Is there anything more?*

That's a pretty straightforward question for Ken Lay, the new CEO. This was his answer:

> *There are absolutely no problems that had anything to do with Jeff's departure. There are no accounting issues. There are no trading issues. No reserve issues. Apparently they say I have plenty of money. No previously unknown problem issues. The company's probably in the strongest and best shape that it's ever been in. There are no surprises. We did file our 10-Q...*

Lay is referring to the 10-Q statement the SEC requires all publicly-traded companies to submit each quarter. It contains the information on the fundamentals of the company. Lay continued:

> *We filed this 10-Q with the SEC a few days ago, and if there are any serious problems, they'd be in there. If there's anything material and we're not reporting it, we'd be breaking the law. We don't break the law.*

In hindsight, we know that the company was indeed breaking the law. But at the time, an investor would have looked at Enron's fundamentals and thought everything was in good shape. They lied big time!

But a chart of the stock's price doesn't lie. Even when a company lies about their numbers to the government, they can't lie about what the market thinks of the stock because it's always reflected in the stock price. That's just one reason it's so important to know how to do both fundamental and technical analysis. Both approaches tell different parts of the same story, a story you need to know.

> **KEY POINT!**
>
> ## Technical analysis helps us study the strength of the market
>
> ## The market moves based on supply and demand

Once we know *what* is likely to happen it's natural to want to know *when* it will likely occur.

Whether the news is good or bad, we like to know the details. If I tell my son what is going to happen, like going to the dentist's office, he immediately asks when we will be leaving.

If I tell the kids we're going to take a family trip to visit a Disney resort, they want to know what time we are leaving. Leaving in ten minutes has a completely different value to them than leaving in 10 days.

You will notice that fundamental analysis did much more than just show us the strength of the entity. Now that we have learned a little more about how fundamental analysis works, you can see that it also helps us figure out if we are receiving the value we want for the money we spent on buying shares of a company's stock. It helps us diagnose problems with policies—on the personal level, the corporate level, or the sovereign level. It can help us see both sides of the coin, such as when you compare what your mortgage looks like on you financial statement and what it looks like on your bank's financial statement. In looking at your mortgage from two points of view, it's easy to see the winner and the loser in a transaction. But another thing you might have noticed in the last chapter is that fundamentals can give us keen insight into *what* is likely to happen next.

For example, suppose we have been closely watching the sovereign fundamentals of the United States. As the Federal Reserve enacts more quantitative easing, we think about *what* is likely to happen: inflation, an increase of systemic risks, weakening of the dollar, and volatility. All of these are distinct possibilities. In these circumstances, we might consider some investments to guard against volatility and exploit inflation. But *when,* and at *what price point* should we make these investments?

Keeping our eyes on the stock charts and technical analysis strategies can help us know when to make our move. This is true for all types of investments, not just individual stocks. The charts we use in technical analysis show us whether a company's stock price is revving in place, moving up another gear, or has run out of gas.

Technical analysis is the business of looking at the charts to find the right time and place to enter or exit an investment. This is what we're going to delve into more deeply in this chapter.

Let's begin by looking at the forces that can make a stock price move.

Introducing the Market Makers

If you've ever watched a financial news channel or seen some of the electronic signs in Times Square in NYC, then you've probably seen a stock board with ticker quotes.

Like everything else in the world with a price tag on it, the changes in share price depend on supply and demand. The stock market is made up of a vast sea of investors who want to buy and sell stocks. You can probably imagine how the law of supply and demand works in the stock market because it works the same way with everything we buy, from the price of gasoline, to a package of sugar, to car insurance. In any open market, we find that when there are more sellers than buyers, the price goes down. Conversely, when there are more buyers than sellers, the price goes up.

However, when you buy a stock you do not buy it directly from another investor on the other side of the table. It's not a direct transaction like going to the neighborhood fruit stand and giving a local farmer a few dollars for a bushel of peaches. Instead, you buy shares through a middleman called a *market maker* or a *specialist*.

Market Maker

A market maker is a person or firm willing to accept the risk of holding a certain number of shares in a particular company and stands ready to buy and sell shares of stock of that company from and to other investors.

Why are market makers important? They provide a degree of liquidity for the market.

As a stock trader, a logical question to ask is, "If I decide to sell my shares of stock, how do I know there is someone in the market willing to buy them?"

The answer is that you can generally buy or sell shares of stock at any time you want because the market makers are standing by ready to buy and sell at any given time. In fact it is their job to maintain liquidity.

In Chapter 2 we spent some time discussing the fact that one of the things that makes the stock market unique is its high level of liquidity. It's difficult to sell a house or clear a warehouse full of inventory with the click of a button. But stock traders do it every single day—sometimes many times per day. So it's worth spending some time to understand how market makers keep the stock market liquid.

Suppose you have 100 shares of IBM and you want to sell them, how do you know there will be any buyers? Well, one of the features of the markets is that there is always a balance of buyers on one side and sellers on the other.

Let's look at how the market maker maintains this balance. Now let's suppose you want to buy a certain stock. Your first step—after doing your fundamental analysis, of course—is to check the stock quote provided by the market maker. In today's world, getting a stock quote from a market maker is easier than ever before. Unlike decades ago when we had to call a broker, today we can get real-time stock quotes on our personal computers and even on our smart phones.

To buy a stock, you can look at your smart phone and see that the market maker is currently asking $52.17 per share. This is called the *ask price*, which is the price the market maker is willing to sell it for. If you want to sell the same stock, we can see that the market maker is offering to buy it for $52.15 per share. This is called the *bid price*.

Market Maker

Buyers pay the Market Maker's "Ask Price" $52.17	"spread" 2¢	Sellers accept the Market Maker's "Bid Price" $52.15

Do you notice the small difference of $0.02 between the bid price and ask price? This is called the *spread*, and it is how the market maker earns his living. When there are a lot of shares being bought and sold, this spread is usually quite small, as in the example above. But in a situation where there are not many shares being traded, the spread is typically larger.

The market makers will always buy your stocks and they will always have stocks to sell you. Their goal is volume, and by adjusting their prices, they can achieve volume whether the price is shooting up or falling like a rock.

KEY POINT!

Market Makers stand ready to buy and sell shares of a given security.

This provides investors with a degree of liquidity in the market.

Market makers keep the balance between selling and buying. If there are too many buyers, they take the price up until it reaches a point where sellers are willing to part with their shares. If there are too many sellers, with everyone trying to get rid of a stock, they take it right down until some people start saying, "Gee, that's cheap; maybe it's worth the risk at this price."

This is why you want to learn more about technical analysis: So you can easily decipher the story in the price charts. A large, strong company, like Procter & Gamble or Walmart, might record increased earnings. The share price goes up. The improvement in earnings is not what directly moves share price, however. What directly moves the price is the increase in actual buying of the stock, the effect of supply and demand. In this example, the price movement is indirectly connected to fundamentals, but this is not necessarily always the case. Prices can move for a variety of reasons—news, a rumor, a tip in the media, profit-taking, short-covering, group rotation...or for no obvious reason at all.

KEY POINT!

Stock charts tell the story of supply and demand which may or may not correlate with fundamental analysis

---

Market makers are not concerned with how high or how low a stock's price goes. Their concern is to keep a balance between buyers and sellers to maintain the spread between the ask and the bid prices. This can be disconcerting for those determined to hold shares for the long term. There comes a point when you realize that the long-term prospects of a stock price depend on other investors being willing to pay more for it than you did. People like low prices—not high ones. So a company must sustain enough growth over your investing timeline of 30 years or so to maintain a price/earnings ratio that can justify higher prices fundamentally. Then you must rely on other investors to actually place the orders to drive the price higher technically.

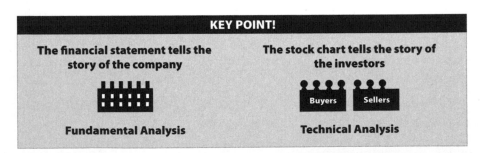

Types of Trends

Through fundamental analysis we saw how to read the story of a company through its financial statements. Now we're going to read the story of a stock through the behavior of investors and their effect on the stock price over a period of time.

Up Trend   **Down Trend**   **Sideways Trend**

An *uptrend* occurs when there is a trend of high demand and low supply of a stock—the price goes up to persuade those holding the stock to sell.

A *downtrend* occurs when there is a trend of high supply and low demand—so the price drops to persuade investors to buy the stock.

Sometimes a stock price doesn't really go up or down much at all, so we refer to the trend as *sideways* or *stagnant*.

It's important to note that technical analysis can be useful to tell the story of supply and demand for any market. We can also use charts to monitor the story of anything that has a price that is affected by supply and demand. It's common for investors to look at charts of commodities like oil, corn, or gold to name just a few. We can look at real estate prices and determine trends. You can study trends in an index such as the Dow or the NASDAQ, or various other markets. Some people think that learning technical analysis is just for stock traders. Nothing could be farther from the truth. Robert Kiyosaki is a huge advocate of learning technical analysis regardless of the asset class or classes you're investing in because investors must understand trends! All four of the assets classes—business, real estate, commodities, and paper—have trends. Thus, technical analysis is vital for investors of all types. Commodity investors can use charts to track the price of everything from gold to oil to soy beans. Business owners can identify trends in their sector. Real estate investors can use charts to track the supply and demand for rentals, housing prices, employment trends, and more. But one thing is common to all these stories of supply and demand: tracing what prices people are willing to pay. At what point do people say "no" and resist paying the price, and at what point will they say "yes" and support a certain price?

Support and Resistance

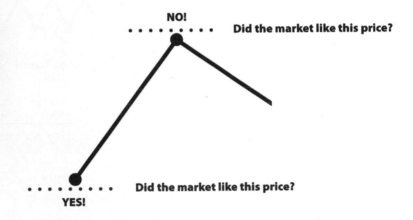

For the following examples in understanding more aspects of technical analysis, let's look at a fictional company named ACME.

You can see, when the share price of ACME is at the level of the bottom dotted line, it starts to go up. At that point, investors are saying "yes" to the price, they think it provides good value. They are in *support* of buying at that price. In fact, we know that more investors want to buy at that price than those who want to sell because the market maker begins to move the price up. The bottom dotted line indicates a *support line* where people are willing to buy the stock at that price. And they continue saying "yes" to the price...right up until it reaches a level where they aren't comfortable anymore. That's when they change and say "no" to the price. At this point, the market maker drops the price because there are not enough buyers at the dotted *resistance line* at the top. This is the price at which buyers *resist* any further price increase, and the price goes down.

Investors are very interested to see points of support and points of resistance because they represent where attitudes change. By looking at these points on a chart we can see where and when investors changed their view on what they were willing to pay.

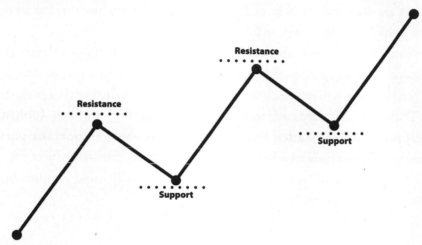

In the chart above, we can see the price going up and down. Notice that in this case, when the price turns downward, the falling price does not drop all the way to the original support level. Over time, the stock chart tells us when investors have a new opinion on what the price should be. So, when we look at a stock chart, there are new levels of support and new levels of resistance that appear as we watch the story unfold.

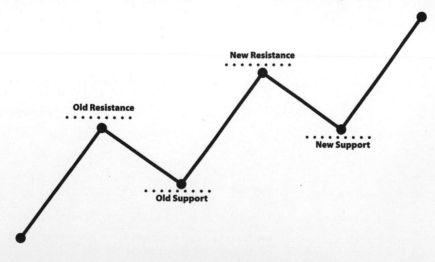

In the chart above we can see a new higher level of support. This is where investors see the price of ACME as a bargain and begin buying again. This buying at a higher price formed a new support level.

As buyers outnumber sellers, there will be a surge in the price until it reaches another resistance level. If at some point buyers lose interest in the stock at higher prices, they will begin selling again.

Note in the example above that with each surge, the support levels and resistance levels moved a little higher. Through these ups and downs, we can see the story's main plotline of a general uptrend during this period.

There are hundreds of technical indicators but, for me, **looking at support and resistance levels is one of the most important parts of technical analysis**. And the more you practice, the better you get at analyzing them until you find that you automatically build support and resistance lines into any chart you study.

Swing Highs and Swing Lows

Another way to look at the chart is as if it were a sketch of mountain peaks and valleys. We have a number of mountain peaks, where the price met with *resistance*. We call these *swing highs*. Where the price drops to its *support* levels we have valleys, which we call *swing lows*.

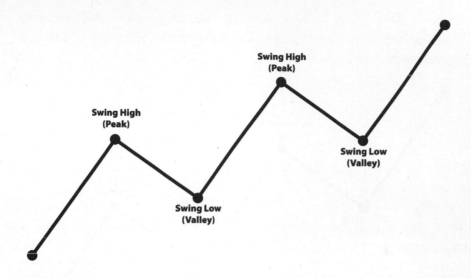

To say that a stock is in an ***uptrend*** might seem pretty easy. But professional stock investors are picky and get very specific about what constitutes an uptrend. For a stock to be considered in an uptrend, both the mountain peaks and the valleys must be getting higher. So an uptrend is a series of upward-trending swing highs *and* upward-trending swing lows. Each swing high is higher than the last and each swing low is higher than the last—higher swing highs and higher swing lows.

KEY POINT!
Uptrend
Chart shows higher swing highs and higher swing lows

The uptrend tells us that investors like ACME shares and they are willing to pay more and more to buy them. Technical analysts love to spot breakouts of new swing highs quickly so they can position themselves to profit from a sustatined uptrend. They also watch for the first time a price fails to achieve a higher swing high. If the stock fails to make a higher swing high, the uptrend is over, for the time being.

In fact, if the market shows resistance and the price fails to form a higher mountain peak, that is often the first evidence that a downtrend could be developing. If, after a stock fails to achieve a higher swing high and then descends to form a lower swing low, the stock is now in a **downtrend**.

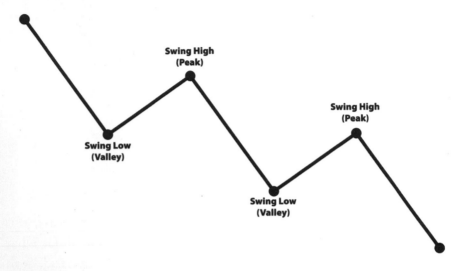

With a sustained **downtrend** we can see a series of lower swing lows and lower swing highs. Just as in the case of an uptrend, technical analysts are very keen to spot trends early so they can position themselves to either gain protection from the downtrend or to profit from it.

KEY POINT!
Downtrend
Chart shows lower swing highs and lower swing lows

Finally, we can have a **sideways market** where the stock is sluggish and the swing lows and swing highs remain at the same level.

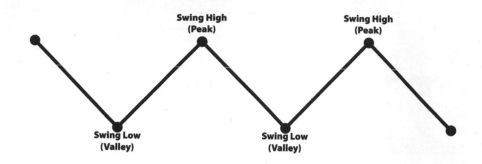

Go with the Trend

A very common approach for technical analysis is to apply the analysis of trends to the broader market. We can look at a chart of the S&P 500 or the NASDAQ and ask ourselves, "Are investors buying stocks right now, or selling them?" The trend is the reality of the situation, and we want to go with the trend.

Before investors look at individual stocks, they first identify the broad market trend. After they see the overall trend of the market, they can then find individual investments that match the same trend.

You can't change the fundamentals or technicals. You can't control the trend. You cannot force a stock price to go up. The stock price is beyond your control.

But you have complete control over your own strategy as to how to position yourself in the market. You can decide when to enter, when to pull out, and whether to *go short* or *go long*. These terms will be explained in detail in the chapter on cash flow, but basically, by *going short*, you have as many opportunities to make money from a downtrend as you have from *going long* in an uptrend.

BUILD ON IT

**PILLAR #2: TECHNICALS
The trend is your friend.**

KEY POINT!

**Investors want to be in harmony with the trend
"The trend is your friend"**

Since we want to be in harmony with the trend, we need to be aware of when it changes. And technical analysis helps signal when the changes occur. Many people, however, get into the bad habit of thinking they can perfectly predict the future from patterns in the charts. They start saying, "I know this is going to happen." But none of us can predict the future perfectly. A better way to think of using technical analysis is in terms of "likelihood."

By reading the charts, you are using information to help develop a strong idea of what is most likely to happen. But reading charts isn't like a carnival fortuneteller who tells you that you will soon meet the man or woman of your dreams. It's more like a weather forecaster who gives you the probability of whether or not it will rain tomorrow. The forecaster doesn't predict the future. Instead, the forecaster informs us of what is likely to happen based on several metrics at his disposal.

The Continuing Trend

Let's look at the story of ACME company again and, by following its chart, see if we can identify a point at which it's likely for the trend to change direction:

We can see in the figure above that after ACME backs off its high price, it reaches a new higher *support level* where investors feel it's a good value for the price. They decide not to wait until it goes down to the previous bargain support level. They now see ACME as a bargain and they begin buying, forming a new and higher support level.

As we can see from the previous rise in price, investors said "no" when it hit a certain price point. With this new upswing, the question we must ask ourselves is whether investors will continue buying through that previous *resistance level* or will they stop again.

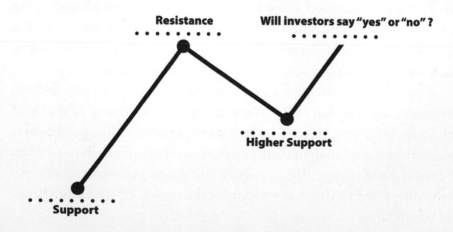

At this point, we don't have enough information to make a good decision. We don't yet know what's likely to happen. Remember that an uptrend means a higher swing high in addition to the higher swing low. This is a situation where we wait for the market to show us what investors are thinking based upon how they act. Their buying or selling behavior will soon tell us the trend of the chart.

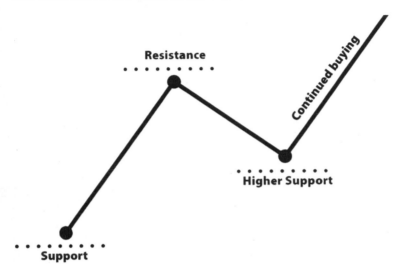

We can see that investors have pushed the price of ACME through the resistance level. We can also see that this stock fits the criteria for an uptrend by hitting a new level that's higher than the previous swing high. No matter where it meets a new resistance level, we'll have a higher *swing high*, and we have also had a higher *swing low*. What we can say is that right now investors are buying it higher and right now they're willing to push it to new levels.

If we follow the trend, we would position ourselves to benefit from the continuation of that trend. You will enjoy profits as long as the trend continues. Of course, this uptrend could end at any time. The good news is that with technical analysis there are often warning signs to show us when the trend could change. The important thing is to have our eyes open to the reality of the situation as we wait for the right time to exit or change our position.

When Does No Mean NO?

Okay, we've been talking about a lot of complicated financial stuff, but let's move to a really simple example because the financial world is just like the real world. The same psychology that drives our personal lives drives the business world—just on a larger scale.

In my life, as you might guess, March is a very special month. It's a month of brackets and excitement. It has been for as long as I can remember. But whereas March Madness used to mean running and jumping and burning off calories faster than I could get them into my body, these days it means my couch, my TV, and Ben & Jerry's ice cream. That trio has become more than a habit for me, it's become a hallowed tradition.

I'd been trying to drop a few pounds for a while, and I'd enlisted my wife's help. I knew I had to change my March Madness policy if I wanted to see my weight drop. But when she suggested I cut out Ben & Jerry's, I thought, "Why don't you stab me in the heart." But after months of getting nowhere on my own with my weight loss, I'd promised to do what she suggested. My new policy was to listen to her. And even though I made the promise before I'd known the depths of depravity to which she'd sink (No Ben & Jerry's during March Madness? Did she even love me?) I agreed to try.

So we were sitting in our home theater—me and my boys and my wife—watching basketball, and all was right with my world except for the absence of Ben & Jerry's. I decided to see if she would allow a small exception for a special occasion and let me cheat for just one day and have my ice cream.

And she said "No."

But the number one rule of sales is to never take "No" for an answer, and I love sales, so I had a pitch ready. I said, "Aw, come on, please?" And I gave her my best sad eyes.

To my surprise, she gave in said "Okay." She said I'd been so good about sticking to my diet, and she understood my love of March Madness, and it was only once a year...so she totally caved.

But it'd been so long since I'd had any ice cream, the whole carton was gone in less than 20 minutes. I just devoured it. We got to half time and the score was within a possession and I was out of Ben & Jerry's. So I suggested I have some more.

And she said "No."

I tried my best puppy-dog *please.*

Ah, the basketball gods were smiling. My wife said "Yes" again. But again I devoured the ice cream before the buzzer.

The clock ran down. The score was tied. Overtime! And I was out of ice cream again. I decided to press my luck once more. This time my wife said "No, absolutely not, enough is enough!"

If I were to chart my wife's responses, you could see a pattern. She said "No" once and I pushed, and she gave in. She said "No" twice and I pushed, and she gave in. But when I asked that third time, she hit her limit and she dug in. She'd hit her level of very strong resistance. I knew not to ask again.

People often react the same way to high prices.

Now let's look at an example where I'm the one saying "No." Suppose my kids want to stay up past their regular bedtime. While I'm generally a pushover when it comes to my kids, I know they have little league practice early the next morning, so they'll need a good night's rest. When my boys beg me to stay up an extra hour, I gently tell them "No" and explain that they need their rest. Kids are notoriously good salespeople, and sometimes act as if they don't know the meaning of the word *no.*

After my initial "No," the boys try again—and this time give their personal guarantee that they will get up early with smiling faces and be ready to go. Now I give them a more emphatic "No." I still have a smile on my face to let them know I love them, but my tone makes it clear to them that they're not going to change my decision.

Let's look at a chart to see how my sons' agenda failed to advance not just once, but twice.

When my sons run into resistance at the same level, it tells them that I'm 'digging in' and I am much less likely to change my feelings on the matter. The same is true with the market and the price investors will pay.

So a technical analyst might not read too much into a single resistance point on a chart. But if we see resistance occurring at the same point more than once, it tells us that the market has reached a limit for the time being on what investors are willing to pay.

The Double-Top Alert—Two "Nos" Are More Stubborn than One

What happens when buyers backed off at the same resistance level? They have now resisted twice at the same level. Obviously, they are not willing to pay more than that for the stock. For whatever reason, the market does not see value at that price point. This is called a *double top* pattern.

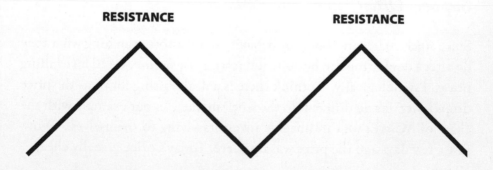

The story of a double top tells us that at the first resistance level, investors answered with a small "no" to the price at that level. After the price heads down and bounces back up again, this time the investors gave an emphatic "NO!" that shows they are serious about it. They are not interested in buying at that price. It's possible, of course, that they could change their minds the next time the price heads to that resistance level. However, since we are using the information and our intelligence to determine the likelihood of a situation, we can be aware that it is now less likely that the stock will achieve a higher swing high in the near future.

KEY POINT!

Charts are not a crystal ball. They indicate what is likely.

But does the double-top pattern by itself tell us that the trend is now going to change? No.

Simply because buyers are saying "no" at a certain price point doesn't mean the trend is changing downward. Again, it's too soon to tell, but it does get our attention, and we certainly can see that a change is more likely. For this reason, a double-top pattern is an alert. Like a fire alarm, it does not guarantee a fire, but it makes us pay attention.

This is a good example of how we can better understand the minds of investors purely through seeing what is happening on the price chart.

Support Often Turns into Resistance

Since stock charts are about the behavior of investors, watching what they do after a double top can be quite interesting. By nature, we all love falling prices. Psychologically, we think there is a deal waiting for us as the price drops lower. It's no different in the stock market. In our example with the chart of ACME, we can imagine investors saying to themselves, "Wow, just a few days ago the price was up there. Today's price is really cheap."

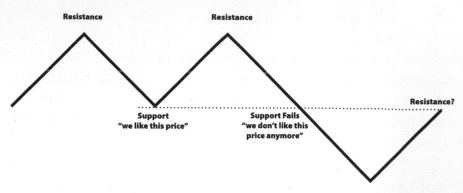

With the price falling below the previous support level, investors now have a very interesting situation in front of them. Typically, they would see a great buying opportunity and begin to buy shares of ACME at this apparently low price level. This, of course, would drive the price back up again. As it reaches the previous support level again, we call this point a little *kiss*. The question is, what kind of a kiss will it be? It could be a *kiss goodbye,* where it bounces off this old support level and it becomes a new resistance level. If this is the case, the price can drop again for a time.

In the example above we can see a full-fledged *kiss goodbye.* This illustrates how the previous support line now becomes a level of resistance. Investors are unwilling to buy above this level and are saying "no." When we see the support level becoming a new resistance level, it helps us see that the trend is truly changing.

There is now a real downward pressure on ACME's stock price. Investors are resisting that price level and, as a result, the price is falling. We have had a lower swing low followed by a lower swing high. Now we can decide to make money by positioning ourselves to profit from the downtrend.

Again, let me stress that chart patterns cannot predict the future. A double top does not mean that the stock will continue to fall. It simply means people said "no" once, and then they said "no" a second time. A double top should get your attention as a warning alarm. It might be a false alarm, but it should at least make you watch the situation more closely.

Suppose you saw the stock in an uptrend and were considering buying the stock to make a capital-gain profit on the increase in price. A double top should cause you to wait and see whether this was a false alarm. As an *alert*, it is helpful for reconsidering which direction the trend is really headed.

At this point, it's important to note that patterns like the double top for the kiss goodbye are merely the tip of the iceberg when it comes to learning about technical analysis.

One of the challenges in writing any book is determining scope. Not only are entire books written on this topic alone, there are entire books written on single aspects of technical analysis. It's less important at this point that you grasp the idea of a *double-top pattern* or a *kiss-goodbye pattern*. It's more important to grasp the general idea that investors can look at a chart and better understand the minds and hearts of investors.

You can imagine the incredible advantage you have as an investor when you can more fully understand what's behind the markets. Whether you're a real estate investor, a commodities investor, a business owner, or a stock investor, this is a skill that's worth having. Earlier in this book we saw that the world economy is in pretty rough shape based on a basic fundamental analysis and the monetary policies and fiscal policies of the larger countries around the world. Our ability to read charts is what will help us see how all of this plays out in the markets.

More Technical Chart Patterns

Now that we understand a few technical analysis concepts such as *double tops* and *support* and *resistance* levels, let's add a few more technical analysis tools we can use to make smarter investment decisions.

My goal is to give you a quick introduction to these patterns that experienced investors use to create profits and steady cash flow for themselves in the market. As you add these patterns and tools to your vocabulary and personal knowledge base, you will be able to recognize them instantly in your own investing. Even more importantly, you will have a base you can build upon for further education in your journey toward investing proficiency.

The Head and Shoulders

As you can see from the chart above, this pattern looks somewhat like a person's 'head and shoulders'...with the head in the middle with a shoulder on each side. It's a common pattern that frequently alerts us to a coming downward trend.

On the next page is an example of a head and shoulders pattern that developed in the U.S. dollar. This chart represents an exchange-traded fund that tracks the value of the U.S. dollar against other currencies.

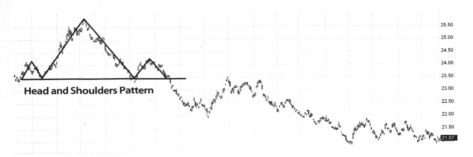

Head and Shoulders Pattern

Looking at the pattern, we can see where the markets have supported the price at the bottom of the pattern, and how they have resisted at the top of the left shoulder, then the top of the head, and then again at the top of the right shoulder. Then, when the investors said "no" to another test of the upper-shoulder level, the price broke below the support and investors sold heavily for a while.

As the chart continues, we need to watch closely to understand the story it is telling us. Remember the rule:

An uptrend is higher swing highs. A downtrend is lower swing lows.

A head and shoulders pattern alerts us that a downtrend has become more likely. If the chart then shows us a lower swing low, that confirms our outlook.

The Double Bottom

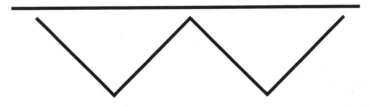

Just as the *double top* can give us an early indication that an uptrend could be reversing soon, the *double bottom* alerts us to the possible end of a downtrend.

And just as the double top looks like the capital letter 'M,' the double bottom looks like a capital 'W,' making it fairly easy to identify. Your response to a double bottom will be the opposite of the way you respond to a double top. This pattern shows the price has bounced back up *twice* from a support level. At this point, many professionals wait for confirmation that it will break through the resistance level. Once it has confirmed that the downward trend is reversing, they put in an order to buy, just above the resistance level.

The Inverse Head and Shoulders

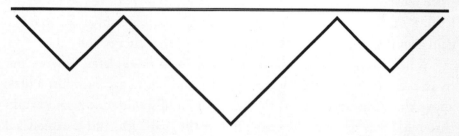

This pattern, which is an upside-down head and shoulders, alerts us to a probable reversal in the downward trend. An *inverse head and shoulders* is typically a bullish pattern that would lead one to place an order to buy this stock when it breaks above the resistance.

The Ascending Triangle

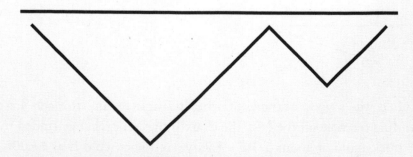

The *ascending triangle* is neither an uptrend nor a sideways trend. We don't have higher swing highs but we do see higher swing lows. Investors continue saying "no" in quick succession, but each time they do they are also saying "yes" at a higher level. The beautiful thing about a pattern like this is that it can't go on forever.

While the resistance level on top is holding steady, the support level below is pushing ever higher. That's why the support trend line isn't horizontal. Instead, we should be able to visualize a straight line with an upward slope. This represents the pressure cooker situation the stock is experiencing, and we are waiting for that pressure to shoot out the top.

There is no guarantee here, as there never can be a guarantee with any price movements, but if I put an entry order to buy above the resistance level, I am losing nothing if it goes through the bottom, and I stand to gain a lot if it shoots through the top with all that energy behind it.

When we get into cash flow, I'll explain in more detail how we put in an order to buy stock. For example, I could put in an entry just a little above that resistance line. If they say "no," and it goes down and breaks through, I was never in the trade. But, if they say "yes "and it explodes, I catch it right there. *Bam!* And I like the idea that when someone has said "no" for so long, if they finally say "yes," I'm in for the ride. Those are really fun to hit.

Gold was a good example of a fun triangle to hit. You can see the ascending triangle on the left. The chart shows an exchange-traded fund that tracks gold at about 1/10th of its value (when gold is at $1,000 an ounce, the fund is at $100). Buyers kept saying "no" for a long time at $1,000 an ounce, but when that resistance eventually broke they were saying "yes" at ever-higher levels, and the resistance level rose rapidly. *Bam!*

Much More You Can Learn

There are many other technical chart patterns and indicators available to help us better understand what is happening on the charts. There is much more available to learn about *candle patterns* and even special indicators that have been created to use with your technical analysis. Of course, this book is designed to introduce technical analysis to beginner-level investors. Delving deeply into the full library of these tools is beyond the scope of our conversation in this book.

For a more in-depth discussion of these indicators, you can request information on my in-depth online training programs at www. stockmarketcashflow.com

We've covered a lot of ground in this chapter. We learned some new concepts and ways to understand what happens to a stock price in the market.

Remember, we can't control which direction the markets go. But we can intelligently monitor them and watch for the patterns that can alert us to possible changes in the market.

Why is learning about fundamentals and technicals so important? Because it's the process of gathering information for our investing. Now that we know ways to gather and analyze this information, we're ready to make money with it. We're ready to learn how to generate cash flow from the market.

Bonus Training!

Let me show you some real–world examples of why cash flow investing is better for most people. Watch this short video here

www.stockmarketcashflow.com

Chapter Summary

Let's review some of the important points of Chapter Five:

1. Technical analysis helps us get information on the strength of the market.

   Prices move based on supply and demand. Stock charts are simply historical records to show investors a picture of the various prices at which a stock was traded during a particular time period. Stock charts can be used to give investors information on anything that has a price: real estate, currencies, stocks, commodities (such as gold and oil), etc.

2. Market makers stand ready to buy and sell shares of a given security.

   The fact that market makers stand ready to buy and sell shares provides a degree of liquidity in the markets. Market makers do not care whether they move prices up or down. They simply match buyers with sellers based on supply and demand.

3. Stock charts tell the story of supply and demand, which may or may not correlate with fundamental analysis.

   Because supply and demand involves speculation and emotion, investors may buy stocks that do not yet have a proven track record. When buying, they hope that the stock will be more valuable in the future. However, they may also sell off shares of a fundamentally sound company because of their nervousness over a possible selling panic.

4. The financial statement tells the story of the company through fundamental analysis, and the stock chart tells the story to investors through technical analysis.

   Investors can use fundamental analysis and technical analysis to make more informed decisions related to how they want to position themselves.

5. An uptrend is created when a chart shows higher swing highs and higher swing lows.

   Professional investors use trend to determining what position to take with a stock.

6. A downtrend is created when a chart shows lower swing highs and lower swing lows.

   If a stock is in a downtrend, investors will generally take a short position, which means they will profit if the stock price falls. If the price changes direction, investors will execute an exit strategy.

7. A sideways trend is created when a chart shows swing highs and swing lows within a range.

8. Investors want to be in harmony with the trend.

   The old adage is that "the trend is your friend." Many professional investors analyze the broad market trend first and then find individual stocks that are in harmony with the broad market trend.

9. Charts are not a crystal ball. They indicate what is most likely to happen.

   Professional technical analysts are like weather forecasters. They're less prone to speak in absolutes and more prone to speak about likelihoods.

Chapter Six

Pillar 3: Cash Flow

The chapters leading up to this one were designed to help you gain the knowledge and understanding of the tools you'll need to make smart investing decisions by finding and understanding valuable information about a company and the trends. As you've learned: Fundamental analysis gives you valuable information about an entity and technical analysis gives you important insights into the minds and hearts of investors to help you keep your finger on the pulse of supply and demand—and determine what is most likely to happen and when.

With those tools in your toolbox, you are now ready to get into the business of how you can position yourself to increase net worth or cash flow from the stock market.

Turning Information into Profit by Positioning

As you take this next step it can be helpful to think of using the first two pillars of fundamental analysis and technical analysis as the *information gathering* phase, and the last two pillars of cash flow and risk management as the *positioning* phase.

KEY POINT!	
First phase is gathering information	**Second phase is determining your position**
Fundamental Analysis **Technical Analysis**	**Cash Flow Strategies** **Risk Management**

The first two pillars of fundamentals and technicals help you to determine your outlook. The last two pillars of cash flow and risk management help you harvest this information and profit by positioning yourself to benefit from what is most likely to occur with certain assets.

The Four Pillars			
Information		Positioning	
Fundamental Analysis	**Technical Analysis**	**Cash Flow**	**Risk Management**
Information on the strength of an entity	Information on market strength or "trend"	Position to benefit from what's likely	Position for sudden change
Financial Statements	**Charts and Indicators**	**Acquire Assets**	**Protect Assets**
Household	Broad market indexes	Long position	Hedge with contracts
Corporation	Assets classes	Short position	Hedge with insurance
Government	Sectors	Net worth position	Exit strategy
Policy	Individual investments	Cash flow position	Position size
Demographics		Leverage by debt	Non-correlated assets
		Leverage by contract	Tax planning / legal

The Education Continuum™

Ignorance ⟶ Awareness ⟶ Competency ⟶ Proficiency

This concept of harvesting information to your benefit is profound because it frees you from having to hope that markets always perform well and having to pray that the economy will be kind to you. The ability to use information, whether it's positive or negative, to one's benefit can mean freedom from the political policies that are beyond your control, dependency on your company for a job, or dependency in a 401(k) program that by and large requires a long-term growth in the market.

It's also worth mentioning that in the information-gathering phase you have no control. You're just an observer. The fundamental and technical details you discover are simply what they are. In the positioning phase, on the other hand, you have total control of how you position your investments to take full advantage of whatever market situation you see. Therefore, you have the responsibility to position yourself as intelligently as possible.

You've probably heard this saying before: "When life gives you lemons, make lemonade." Perhaps the stock-market version of this would be, "When life gives you a bear market, make more money." That is part of the magic of turning any information—good or bad—into profit.

As we move into the second half of this book, we will be covering some of my favorite topics.

- Examples of positioning to make money in any type of market: up, down, or sideways.

- How to more intelligently set investing goals and determine how capital gains and cash flow fit into your plans.

- How the stock and options market can work together for cash flow and risk management.

- One of Warren Buffett's favorite strategies...and one you, too, can learn and master.

Because I want to give you some examples from the real world, I will illustrate a few of them with some of my own trades. I think it's beneficial to see how these trades work in real-life scenarios, not just theory. But it's important that I do this with a word of warning:

WARNING: When I show you my trades, I am NOT recommending that you should trade the way I do. Also, I am not recommending that you trade the same stocks that I do. Remember, my trades are shared only for the purpose of illustrating real-world examples and to assist in your understanding of specific concepts.

There's a big difference between education and advice. And this book operates strictly in the realm of education.

Your goal should be to move along the Education Continuum™. Remember that too many people fall victim to the desire to make a quick buck from a stock tip. Unfortunately, their focus is on making a single transaction that could potentially be a winner. It's unlikely that these people will ever be truly independent. They will always be dependent on others—on people who can give them tips. As your understanding grows, you will begin to know how to make your own trades and take control of your own life.

Investing is for those who take the time to educate themselves, not those who want to gamble their money away. Investing in securities has obvious risks. If I lose money, it's my own fault. Please remember that same lesson for yourself.

Before you take a position in the market, remember that not all income is created equal.

When most people set their investing goals, they think very little about the fact that different positions would bring about different results. All money is not created equal. For example, in the United States, the government will look at money earned from working at a job much differently than the same amount of money earned from investing. Money earned from a job or as a small business owner is labeled *earned income*. Money earned in a long-term stock portfolio by buying a stock low and selling high will be labeled as a *capital gain*. In the United States, as of this writing, earned income can be taxed up to 39 percent. But capital gains can only be taxed up to 15-20 percent. Thus, all money is not equal.

Almost every country taxes the money you earn based upon one or more of three categories: *earned income, portfolio income*, and *passive income*. As you set your financial goals, it's essential that you use good tax planning and strategize to earn your income in such a way that you receive maximum tax benefit. To learn more about this, I highly recommend Rich Dad Advisor Tom Wheelwright's book *Tax-Free Wealth*. I've heard Tom say that with the right tax planning and the right positioning, people can make almost any income they earn passive income, with the exception of money that is earned at a job.

For the purposes of this book, however, I want to separate the positions we can take in the stock and options market into three different but very important categories: capital gains, cash flow, and hedges.

KEY POINT!

In the stock or options market, an investment can serve up to 3 different purposes:

Capital gain
Cash flow
Hedge

If you have been a Rich Dad student, you are probably familiar with Robert and Kim Kiyosaki's educational board game, *CASHFLOW® 101.* One of the primary lessons taught in this game is the ability to tell the difference between an opportunity that will produce capital-gain income and an opportunity that will produce cash-flow income.

Positioning with Assets

When I teach classes all over the world, people are always asking me for advice: "Andy, should I buy gold?"

My response to questions like this is usually pretty irritating to those people who simply want to be told what to do: "Well, I can't give you financial advice, because I'm just your teacher. But I'm curious...what do you want your gold to do?"

"I just want to make money," they reply.

These folks don't understand that what I'm really asking them is whether they want to buy gold for capital gain, cash flow, or as a hedge against a falling currency.

A more sophisticated investor would understand that I'm not trying to irritate them. It's just that depending upon the fundamentals and technicals of the day, gold might be a wonderful hedge against inflation but a very poor cash flow vehicle. So if the person wants to buy gold to become financially independent, then the answer is probably *no*, because gold is unlikely to provide a monthly passive income that exceeds expenses. Gold is like the proverbial golden egg. It might go up and down in value, but it's not going to produce new golden eggs.

However, if the person has a large cash position and is worried about losing the value of that cash to inflation, then the answer might be *yes*... it might make sense for a certain amount of their wealth to be placed in precious metals.

Obviously, most of the people I come in contact with are at the beginning of their investing education. Learning personal fundamental analysis and using a personal financial statement to set goals is a great place to start.

Taking Control

Remember that risk is related to control. One of the frustrating things about buying a stock is that you have no control over how it moves. In our discussion of fundamentals and technicals we saw this very clearly. If you refuse to adjust your position, then once you buy that stock you are at the mercy of how the market moves it.

Long-term investors like those who have 401(k) accounts cannot control whether their account value goes up or down. They just hope it's bullish, because hope is all they have to hold onto. They are at the mercy of the fundamentals and technicals and lack the skills to improve their position. When life gives these folks a lemon they don't know how to make lemonade.

KEY POINT!			
You *can't choose* what the information tells you		**You *can choose* what position to take**	
Fundamentals (Financial statements)	**Technicals** (Stock charts)	**Cash Flow** (Long vs short)	**Risk Management** (Insured vs not)

On the other hand, when you use information from fundamentals and technicals, you are gathering the details you need to gain some control through positioning. Even though we can never control how a market's price will move, we can choose how to position ourselves to manage risk to whatever level we're comfortable with. And you can adjust these positions whenever you want. If you develop a willingness to adjust your position as the information changes, it will bring you a wealth of new opportunities. It doesn't matter if the economy is bad or if jobs are scarce. It doesn't matter if the market is moving up, down, or just sputtering sideways. You will always have opportunities to generate reliable income in any market conditions.

Let's look at just the cash flow section of the table:

Cash Flow		
Acquire Assets		
Long position	Net worth position	Leverage by debt
Short position	Cash flow position	Leverage by contract

Depending on the fundamentals and technicals, you will have some decisions to make. Will you take a *long position*, a *short position* or a *neutral position*? Will you position yourself for a nice capital gain to grow your net worth, or do you want a position that will deliver monthly cash flow? Do you want to be in a position of leverage? If you do, then will you use debt or a contract?

Long and Short Positions

As a general rule, if the fundamentals and technicals suggest that something is going up in value, you want to own it. When investing, owning something—anything—means you are in a *long position*.

This holds true with anything you buy and take ownership of:

- If you buy some gold you are *long gold*.

- If you buy some stock you are *long the stock*.
- If you have U.S. currency in a savings account you are *long the dollar*.

As the information from fundamentals and technicals change, you may wish to change your position as well. So you would enter a long position by buying a stock, and then exit that long position by selling the stock:

- You *enter a long position* by buying the gold, and then *exit your long position* by selling the gold.
- You *enter a long position* by buying the stock, and then *exit your long position* by selling the stock.
- You *enter your long position* on the U.S. dollar by receiving dollars by exchanging something for the dollars like goods or services, and you *exit your long position* on the dollar when you spend the dollars on something else.

BUILD ON IT

**PILLAR #3: CASH FLOW
A long position is when you buy it; you exit a long position when you sell it.**

Everybody knows what it's like to be in a long position. If you have money in the bank you are in a long position on cash. If you have an automobile you have a long position on that automobile.

Taking a short position is less understood and even misunderstood by the average person. When my first stock mentor explained to me how to take a short position and what it meant, I have to admit that I didn't fully understand it right away. It's counterintuitive.

KEY POINT!
Long Positions

You enter a *long position* when you:	You exit a *long position* when you:
Buy something and you own it	**Sell it**

Let's begin by looking at three important facts of taking a short position:

1. You are going to position yourself to make money on something that is falling in value.

2. You are going to sell something that doesn't belong to you.

3. You are going to change the order of buying and then selling—to doing the exact opposite. In other words, you are going to sell something first and then buy it later. (I don't know about you, but this made my brain freeze up when I was first introduced to this concept. But there was a large part of me that wanted to understand this. I was interested to see how investors could take such a position and profit from it!)

As stated previously, if we think something is going up in value then we can enter a *long position* by *purchasing* the item and then exit that *long position* by *selling* the item. So it does make a little bit of sense that if we believe the item going down in value that we should enter a *short position* by *selling* the item and then exit the *short position* by *buying* the item back.

But how does someone sell something they don't own? The answer is simple: First borrow from one individual and then sell it to another individual to *enter your short position*. After the item has fallen in value then you can *exit your short position* by buying the item back at the new (and hopefully lower) price and return it to its owner.

KEY POINT!			
Long Position		**Short Position**	
You enter a *long position* when you:	You exit a *long position* when you:	You enter a *short position* when you:	You exit a *short position* when you:
Buy something and you own it	Sell it	Borrow something and then sell it	Buy it back and return it

I want to repeat that, as a teacher, I have the opportunity to teach this concept to thousands and thousands of people. I'd say less than one in a hundred fully understand what entering a short position is all about prior to their first lesson.

BUILD ON IT

PILLAR #3: CASH FLOW
A short position is when you borrow something and sell it; you exit a short position when you buy it back and return it.

To further help you understand, I want to give you a few small examples of short positions. If you have a little trouble getting your head around this, simply review the examples again. Or you can spend some time going through a little more free training I've created for you at **www.stockmarketcashflow.com** where you can watch a free video presentation that breaks down short positions in a way that supplements the detail in this or any book.

> **Bonus Training!**
> For many people, watching a video explanation of shorting helps them better understand this concept.
>
> To watch, go to
> www.stockmarketcashflow.com

Most U.S. Real Estate Investors Have a Short Position on the U.S. Dollar

Even a basic look at fiscal policy, monetary policy, sovereign fundamentals, and technical analysis on a large scale suggest that the value of the U.S. dollar is likely to decline over the long term. In fact, take a look at the last 30 years and it's pretty likely you'll find yourself wishing you had taken a short position on the US dollar. So how can we position ourselves most effectively if this indeed happens?

If you decide to save money, remember that you are in a long position on the U.S. dollar. You'll acquire your U.S. dollar in exchange for some goods or some services when the dollar's value is high. If you go shopping today with your dollars, you could buy a lot of great things (and 30 years ago you could have bought even more for the same amount of cash). But if you maintain your long position in the dollar (saving money under the mattress) and the dollar loses value in the future, suddenly you won't be able to buy as many nice things with the same amount of money. That's what happens when the dollar loses its value over time.

Let's suppose you decide to take a short position in the U.S. dollar. Remember, to take a short position we would borrow the money and then exchange it for something that is valuable, such as real estate. One of the advantages of borrowing money in the United States is that often the loan can be acquired at a fixed rate, which means you'll have the same monthly payment that will never change. As the dollar loses value it takes more dollars to buy valuable things. Food prices will go up because it will take more dollars to buy the valuable food. Clothing prices will go up because it takes many more weak dollars to purchase valuable clothing. The same is true with shelter. If the dollar loses value, then whoever is renting your home needs to give you more of their dollars to compensate you for allowing them to stay in your home. With each year that passes, your monthly loan payment to the bank won't change as you return the borrowed dollars to the bank. However, those dollars are now worth much less than when you initially borrowed them.

When house flippers and weekend-warrior real estate investors speak, they always talk about the houses. They talk about re-habing and foreclosure auctions and such. When I hear professional real estate investors like Kenny McElroy and Robert Kiyosaki speak, it's almost always about debt, the decline of the dollar, and taxes. They almost never talk about housing! Why? Because a person who buys real estate with all cash is a LONG position in real estate. But a person who uses debt to buy real estate is in a SHORT position on the dollar! Many real estate investors fail to see that other side of the coin! So the fundamentals and technicals of the dollar are as important to them as the fundamentals and technicals of the real estate market.

Perhaps a better word to use than "sell" might be the word "trade." When you sell, you are trading something you have for dollars.

Shorting the Dollar with Real Estate	
You enter a *Short position* when you:	**You exit a *Short position* when you:**
Borrow dollars from the bank and sell or "trade" your dollars for a house	Get the dollars back from your tenant and return less valuable dollars to the bank

The worst thing that can happen to an investor in a long position is for the item they are holding to lose value. Conversely, that means that the worst thing that can happen to an investor in the short position is that the item could increase in value during the time they have borrowed it.

Imagine what would happen to our real estate investment if the dollar were to increase in value. That means prices would fall because dollars would have more purchasing power. In a situation where it takes one thousand "weak" dollars to purchase one month's rent, it might only require five hundred "strong" dollars to purchase one month's rent. Why? Because a strong dollar has more purchasing power than a weak dollar. Yet the monthly payment for the mortgage remains constant. Thus, a strengthening dollar could place the real estate investor in a position of negative cash flow if he's using debt as a lever.

We take a short position in the stock market by simply borrowing shares of stock from our brokerage and then selling them on the open market to receive cash. Once the stock falls in price, we can then buy those shares at a lower price on the open market and then return the borrowed shares to the brokerage and pocket the cash we earned.

Shorting a Share of Stock	
You enter a *Short position* when you:	**You exit a *Short position* when you:**
Borrow a share of stock from the brokerage. Sell or "trade" your share on the open market.	Buy the share of stock back. Return the share to the brokerage.
Sell $50 1- Borrow a share from brokerage $40 2- Sell the borrowed share at $50	$50 1- Buy the share back at $40 **Buy** $40 2- Return the share
You now have $50 and owe the brokerage a share of stock	**You now have a $10 profit**

Short positions have their own risks, of course. If you are in a long position and the stock goes to zero, it can be devastating. But if you are in a short position, the stock has no limit on the upside—which could be even more devastating. Remember: if you want to go deep into short positions, then visit my website and view the free online class on short positions.

More Education on Short Positions
www.stockmarketcashflow.com

Take an Inventory of Your Assets. How Are You Positioned?

As you ask yourself the question about what kind of money you want to generate from your investments, I recommend looking at your income statement and balance sheet for guidance. Use the understanding you have gained in this book to do your own personal fundamental analysis. Then you will better understand what kind of investments you want and how you want them to change your financial statement.

KEY POINT!

Investing goals should grow out of your financial statement.

How you position yourself in your investments will have a bearing on the numbers in your financial statement based on what kind of investments you acquire. Do you want to grow your net worth as shown on your balance sheet? Or do you want to increase the monthly cash flow on your income statement?

As you set your goals you might examine where you are currently in terms of your paper assets and whether or not your goals are dependent on capital gains. Are you buying stocks today and then hoping to sell them later at a higher price? Or are your paper assets positioned to deliver steady cash flow month in and month out?

The long-term strategy of buying and holding stocks or mutual funds is all about hoping for growth. This may help your net worth in the long run if the market accommodates you, but doesn't provide you with reliable cash flow to add to your income statement every month. Keep in mind the difference between a golden goose and a golden egg. A golden egg strategy is to gather lots of golden eggs and hope the eggs increase in value. A golden goose strategy is to focus on assets to create new golden eggs all the time.

Obviously, this book is about showing you how you can gain a steady cash flow from the stock market. It's a different way of using the market to your advantage that your friends and family probably don't talk about—simply because, in most cases, they just don't know.

Go back to those goals you set earlier. You probably set a goal of having steady cash flow every month. Odds are you want at least enough cash to cover all your bills. If that's the case, you need to set a target number to shoot for every month.

So let's determine how to create enough cash flow to pay all of your bills every month. Take a moment and write down that number—the amount you need every month to live on. If you don't know that number, stop now and figure it out.

This is your expense number—the dollar amount you need to match or exceed with monthly cash flow to gain your financial independence. This is a much more intelligent way to set your goals for financial freedom than just pouring money into some retirement account and hoping there's enough there to live on when you reach a certain age!

Most people use a job to generate the income they need to meet that expense number every month. Go ahead and challenge that way of thinking. That's what the wealthy do.

If you can identify your investing goal now, then you can make major progress toward building the cash flow you'll need to meet that amount. As your monthly cash flow from the market grows, you will rely less on a job and be confident in your own abilities to generate the money you need.

Imagine how it will feel to free yourself from a 9-to-5 job. All it takes is enough cash flow to replace that employment income and pay your expenses. At that point, you'll see your life in a very different way. Instead of thinking of retiring in 20 years when you have a big pile of money saved, I want you to focus on increasing your cash flow to the point where your assets give you the passive income that meets whatever number you desire.

For our purposes, let's suppose that your monthly number is $10,000. That's what you need to meet your expenses every month. With that goal clearly set, you can then develop a plan to go out and buy some stock and make $1, and then $10, and then $100 dollars...and then keep building your assets to provide you with income from your assets. As you keep following this plan of building your assets, one day you can have a cash flow of $10,000 a month, or more. Suddenly, you realize you've achieved financial independence. At $15,000 in monthly cash flow your lifestyle improves drastically!

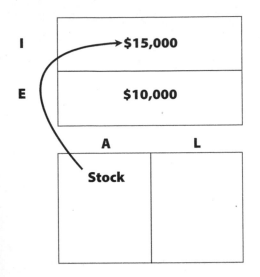

**Passive income > Expenses
= Financial independence**

Note that your net worth is not depicted, at all, in the figure above. Why? Because financial independence isn't about having some massive amount of money in the bank. It's not about having a huge net worth. Instead, financial independence is about having enough cash flow from your assets to live without having to worry about money.

The traditional way of thinking about wealth building is to try and have x-number of millions of dollars at retirement—golden eggs. But there is a better way, a more intelligent way. If you develop the skills to acquire income-producing assets, and then continually learn how to make those assets give you more and more cash, then it doesn't matter what number you are aiming for. At that point, it's simply a matter of growing your assets to reach the number you want. It's essentially the same skill focused on a bigger target.

By thinking about it as a cash-flow goal instead of a net-worth goal, you are fundamentally changing the structure of your financial life. Instead of saving up a lot of money to retire at age 65, you can essentially do whatever you want starting on the day when you have more than enough passive income to cover your expenses. Some people call it early retirement. I call it freedom to live the way we have always dreamed.

Using Leverage

In the market, we use contracts to help us gain leverage. These contracts give a person the choice to buy or sell a stock at a set price, or to simply walk away from the deal completely. In the market, this type of choice is called an *option*.

We can use an option contract to accomplish any of the three investing goals: capital gain, cash flow, or hedge—or any combination of the three.

Rate of Return

Whenever investors put money into an investment, they expect to see their money grow. This growth is called a *return*, and it's simply the profit gained on that investment over a certain period of time. Here's how we calculate it:

KEY POINT!
Rate of return is
Money Out - Money In
————————————————
Money in

In fancy mathematical terms, we can write it like this:

$$(V_f - V_i) \div V_i$$

V_f = Final value of investment

V_i = Initial amount invested

For me, a simpler way to calculate this is to break it up into two simple parts that I can do on a calculator.

First, I count the money pulled out of an investment and then substract the amount of money put into the investment to start with.

Money out − Money in

Then divide by 'Money in':

$$\frac{\text{Money out} - \text{Money in}}{\text{Money in}}$$

Let's do an example and start the investment by buying $100 of stock.
Money in is $100
Then later on you sell it for $110 and get all your money out of the stock.

Money out is $110

To calculate your profit, subtract the money you put in ($100) from the money you pulled out ($110), which gives you a return of $10 on your initial investment.

To calculate the *rate of the return*, you simply divide the return ($10) by the initial amount you put in ($100) to get a return of 0.1 or 10 percent.

When we are comparing the returns of various investment opportunities, the rate of return gives us a good way to evaluate different investments. If one investment generates a return of $300 and another investment has a return of $500, which one is better?

It's hard to tell from those numbers alone because we don't know how much money was initially invested. Seeing the return as a percentage allows us to make apples-to-apples comparisons of different investments.

Increasing the Rate of Return

When people who rely on jobs want to increase their income, they must ask their boss for a raise or look for a different job. Investors, on the other hand, can increase their income by growing the rate of return they get from an investment.

There are two ways to increase the rate of return on an investment:

1. **Have a bigger gain**. This looks simple on paper, but in real life it's not that easy. To double your return, it's unrealistic to think

that you can simply double the money you invest on every trade you make. And since you are somewhat at the mercy of what the market chooses to do, it's impractical to rely on this approach for a regular boost in income.

2. **Reduce the initial investment amount.** Based on the rate of return calculations we just looked at, we can see that if you can find a way to reduce the initial investment as close to zero as possible, then the rate of return can grow very large. In fact, it's possible to grow your rate of return to infinity.

Some Amazing Math

We can see that as we reduce the initial amount of money we risk in an investment the total amount of money we can lose goes down and the potential return goes up. In fact, the ideal amount of money to risk in an investment is actually zero. So what happens to your potential return when the amount of money you put in is zero?

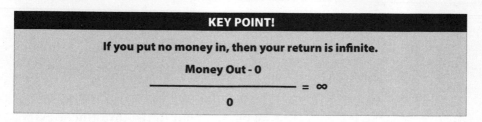

KEY POINT!

If you put no money in, then your return is infinite.

$$\frac{\text{Money Out} - 0}{0} = \infty$$

When I explain this concept of infinite returns to people, I usually get very puzzled looks. Most people believe there's no such thing as an infinite return. Let's look at an example to show you how it works:

<u>Scenario #1</u>

Initial investment = **$100**

Final value = $110

($110 - $100) ÷ $100 = **10 percent rate of return**

Scenario #2

Initial investment = **$10**

Final value = $110

($110 - $10) ÷ $10 = **1,000 percent rate of return**

Scenario #3

Initial investment = **$1**

Final value = $110

($110 - $1) ÷ $1 = **10,000 percent rate of return**

Scenario #4

Initial investment = **10¢**

Final value = $110

($110 - 10¢) ÷ 10¢ = **109,900 percent rate of return**

Scenario #5

Initial investment = **1¢**

Final value = $110

($110 - 1¢) ÷ 1¢ = **1,099,900 percent rate of return**

For all these scenarios, you can see that it is essentially the same investment that grows to $110 for the final value. The difference among the five scenarios is the amount we put in as our initial investment. As we push our initial investment down as low as possible, you can see that the rate of return skyrockets to over one million percent. If we go all the way to zero we get infinity.

Scenario #6

Initial investment = **0**

Final value = $110

($110 - 0) ÷ 0 = **∞ percent rate of return**

Based on these example scenarios, we can see that it's theoretically possible to get a huge rate of return on an investment by reducing the initial investment as low as possible. But the logical question we must ask is this: *Is it really possible to get into an investment at such a low investment amount?* The answer is yes! You can do it by using the principle of leverage.

The Principle of Leverage vs. Hunting for the "Ten Bagger"

Some investors spend a lot of time doing fundamental analysis in the hope of finding a diamond in the rough. They dream about buying a stock for just pennies and then having the stock skyrocket in value. They dream about hitting a big home run that sets them up for life.

Peter Lynch was a famous mutual fund manager for many years with Fidelity. Before his retirement he became known as one of the most successful mutual fund managers in history. I don't know if Peter Lynch would agree, but I feel that being a mutual fund manager was much easier in the bull market of the 1990s than it is today.

In the mid-1980s to the mid-1990s there was a huge influx of capital in the stock market because of legislation that incentivized people to dump money into their 401(k)s. Combined with a robust economy and sensationalism about the birth of the Information Age, computers, and the internet, an individual investor could practically throw darts at a list of stocks on the wall and pick winners. Some of these stocks doubled in price. Others tripled. And some even increased ten-fold. In referring to these companies whose stock prices increased by ten-fold, Peter Lynch coined the phrase "ten bagger."

Today's investor can still occasionally run across a ten bagger. But it seems that they're not nearly as common as they used to be. And in today's volatile market, stocks that achieve ten-bagger status often struggle to stay at those lofty heights. Like a child's toy rocket, they tumble back to earth as fast as they were thrust into the sky.

While it would be nice to think about being able to use fundamental and technical analysis as a crystal ball to tell us which companies are about to become ten-baggers, it's not really a practical way to become a successful investor.

Another way to approach this would be to use leverage. Let's use another real estate example to illustrate this, because it's so easy to understand.

Two friends decide they're going to become real estate investors. The first investor's name is Mr. Cash. He's very afraid of going into debt. He doesn't understand debt very well, so he avoids it like the plague. Mr. Cash purchases a home for $100,000. He puts in $100,000 in cash so he doesn't need a mortgage. Six months later there is a boom in the value of real estate and someone offers Mr. Cash $110,000 for the house. He accepts the offer and sells the house for $110,000. Now let's do our calculation:

$$\text{Money in} = \$100,000$$

$$\text{Money out} = \$110,000$$

$$(\$110,000 - \$100,000) / \$100,000 = 10 \text{ percent}$$

The second investor's name is Mr. Credit. He's actually just as frugal as Mr. Cash, but he understands how debt works. He has a financial education. He is not frivolous by any means, and he is a man of integrity who keeps his promises. So he has proven himself worthy of being extended a lot of buying power and a high credit score. Because he has a great command of credit, he only needs to put $10,000 of his own money into the home as a down payment and he allows the bank to provide the other $90,000.

When the market offers him $110,000 for his house, he can give the bank back the $90,000 he borrowed and he gets to keep additional $20,000 for himself. Let's see how his transaction compares to Mr. Cash's:

$$\text{Money in} = \$10,000$$

$$\text{Money out} = \$20,000$$

$$(\$10,000 - \$20,000) / \$10,000 = 100 \text{ percent}$$

What is so powerful about this simple example is that we began with two homes purchased at the same price and later sold for the same amount of profit. The key point here is to understand that one investor received a 10 percent return on his money while the other investor doubled his money. This illustrates that if an investor can learn how to position himself with leverage, he can receive an extraordinary return on his money based on the same market moves. You are about to see how this can be done in the stock market without using any debt.

KEY POINT!
Two ways to go for bigger returns

Try to find the "ten bagger"	Reduce your initial investment
(Get lucky)	(Use leverage)

In the case of real estate, professional investors use debt as the lever. But there's an important distinction to make here. It wasn't the fact that the investor used debt that created the leverage, but the fact that he decreased his initial investment. If you can find a way to decrease the initial investment required to take control of an asset, you've achieved a position of leverage whether you use debt or some other means.

The options market allows investors to reduce the amount of money required to take control of an investment. A bonus benefit is that this leverage does not require us to take on any obligations of debt. Like debt, many people mistakenly attach a negative connotation to options. But the key is not to approach options with fear, but with respect.

Most investors understand the basic concept of *going long*, which is buying a stock at current market price based on good fundamental and technical analysis in anticipation that it will increase in value. Buying stocks at market price, however, can get expensive—especially if we want to buy a lot of shares. That's why investors who become properly educated know how to use the *leverage* available in the stock market through buying or selling *stock options*.

Leverage and Options

The principle of leverage allows us to accomplish big things with just a little effort. Have you ever tried to steer an old car without power steering? It can be a little difficult and requires strength to turn the wheel. A power steering unit makes it almost effortless to keep your car heading the right direction. Pulling an old nail out of a piece of wood with your bare hands is almost impossible. But when you use the claw end of a hammer pressed against the wood, it pops out almost effortlessly. Using leverage intelligently can make life a lot easier for us.

It's useful to remind ourselves just how powerful the concept of leverage is. Archimedes famously said, "Give me a lever long enough and a fulcrum on which to place it, and I shall move the world."

Regardless of where you stand currently, related to using leverage, the possibilities are limitless. They are literally infinite. It's a shame that this concept is not taught properly in school, for it is one of the keys that can allow people to move from poverty to affluence, and from survival to abundance. It's worth studying and practicing.

In the stock market, we have a very unique kind of leverage available to us in the form of *options*. With options, we are not buying or selling a stock. Instead, an option is an agreement—with another trader through a market maker—that gives us the right to buy or sell a certain stock at a pre-determined price.

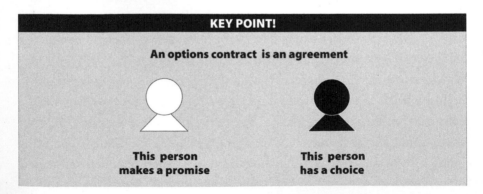

KEY POINT!

An options contract is an agreement

This person makes a promise

This person has a choice

Here's an analogy to help you understand how options work:

The owner of a tailor shop has just put a new tuxedo on display with a price tag of $1,000. You happen to be walking by the store and see the suit in the front window. It's one of the best-looking tuxedos you've ever seen, and you're interested in it. As you go into the store, you're already thinking about pulling out $1,000 and buying the suit on the spot because you think you could turn around and sell it for a good profit later.

As you approach the store owner, however, you have an idea. You decide to use the principle of leverage. Instead of buying the suit right now, you ask the owner to put it on layaway for you (also known in the U.K. as putting it on reserve). By putting it on layaway, you're asking the merchant to hold the tuxedo for you at the price of $1,000. The owner agrees and writes down this agreement on an invoice, you shake hands with him, and you *strike a deal* with him at $1,000. Even if the store owner decides to raise the price of the tuxedo the next day, you're still locked in to buy it at the $1,000 price, if you so choose.

They "strike a deal" at $1,000

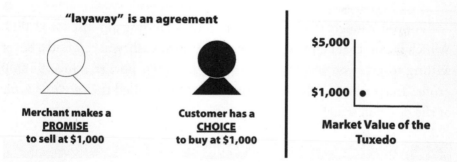

"layaway" is an agreement

Merchant makes a
PROMISE
to sell at $1,000

Customer has a
CHOICE
to buy at $1,000

$5,000

$1,000

Market Value of the Tuxedo

With that layaway paper in your hand, you have a choice—an option. You can go back to the shop before the agreed-upon deadline and buy that tuxedo for $1,000 or you can decide to walk away from the deal. The merchant, however, has an obligation. He's given you a promise. If you come back to buy, he must sell it to you for $1,000, even if he has raised the price for other customers.

After you have put it on layaway, suppose George Clooney is spotted at some red-carpet event wearing that same tuxedo. Orders for this tuxedo begin flooding in from Hollywood and New York. The store owner quickly realizes that he needs to raise the price of the tuxedo to maximize his profits, so it quickly shoots up to $5,000.

They "strike a deal" at $1,000

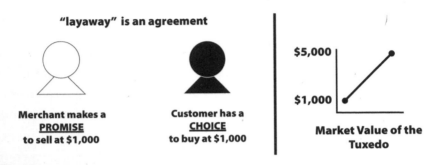

"layaway" is an agreement

Merchant makes a
PROMISE
to sell at $1,000

Customer has a
CHOICE
to buy at $1,000

Market Value of the Tuxedo

**Since you can buy from the merchant for $1,000,
and sell to the market for $5,000,
this agreement is now worth $4,000!**

For you, though, the merchant has made a binding promise for $1,000. Which means that before you even fork over the cash, you can find a buyer willing to give you $5,000 for the suit and then pocket a nice $4,000 profit. That extra $4,000 in the tuxedo's value is called the *intrinsic value* of the deal you struck.

KEY POINT!
"Intrinsic value" is the difference between the price at which you can buy and what the market will pay. **Example: If you can buy at $1,000 and the market will pay you $5,000, the intrinsic value is $4,000.**

In this situation, we can see that it would have been risky to immediately buy the tuxedo for $1,000 and then hope there is a buyer available later willing to buy it from you. We can see that the power in this transaction isn't in the tuxedo. The power is in your option contract. Notice that when the value of the tuxedo increased, so did the value of your agreement.

At first your agreement was nothing special. You could by the suit for $1,000, but so could anyone else.

Agreement has no intrinsic value because anyone can buy at $1,000

Now notice how the value of your contract increased as the value of the tuxedo went up.

Agreement has $4,000 intrinsic value because you buy at $1,000

The $4,000 of intrinsic value comes from your ability to buy the tuxedo at a very low price because of your contract with the tailor. The exciting thing is that to put that $4,000 in your pocket, you don't ever need to go to the tailor again. In fact, you don't even need to go through the hassle of buying that suit and then delivering it to your buyer. All you need to do is to sell your contract. Your agreement is worth $4,000 in cash to any one of the many people in the market who desperately want that tuxedo.

Let's look at the transaction again to calculate your rate of return:

- Money out = $4,000

- Money in = 0

You've made $4,000, but what was your initial investment. Zero.

Suppose you had bought that suit for $1,000 and sold it for $5,000. That's still a good rate of return:

$$(5,000 - 1,000) \div 1,000 = 400 \text{ percent}$$

Earlier I said cash flow is about positioning ourselves. The following diagram helps us compare two different positions we could take on the suit. If we compare these two strategies we can see two dramatically different results.

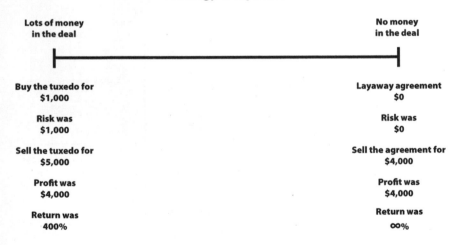

Strategy Comparison

Lots of money in the deal	No money in the deal
Buy the tuxedo for $1,000	Layaway agreement $0
Risk was $1,000	Risk was $0
Sell the tuxedo for $5,000	Sell the agreement for $4,000
Profit was $4,000	Profit was $4,000
Return was 400%	Return was ∞%

This is a simple example to show you how a simple agreement can work to reduce the initial amount of money you put into the investment to achieve a position of leverage.

Notice how you were able to reduce the initial amount of money you put in to zero without going into debt.

It's important to note that you don't have to reduce the amount of money put into the deal all the way to zero to receive a great benefit. In fact, if the merchant would ask you to give them $400 to hold the tuxedo at the thousand-dollar price, you would have still received a far better return with less money at risk with a layaway agreement than actually purchasing the suit for a thousand dollars and then trying to sell it later.

Stock Options

Now let's look at a stock market example. Suppose you are looking to buy a particular stock at $50 per share. You've done your fundamental analysis, you've done the technical analysis, and you think the stock is likely to go up.

**Market value
of the stock**

The next question is: How will you best harvest a profit with that information? How will you decide to position yourself for the greatest benefit?

The most common path for the typical investor would be to purchase shares of the stock. Perhaps someone might buy 100 shares at $50 each. When they do, they risk losing up to $5,000 if the stock does poorly or the company goes bankrupt.

Another possibility is to buy the *option* for that stock. Perhaps you want to establish a position of leverage. Just like when you put that tuxedo on layaway for a certain period of time, you can do the same thing on shares of stock with a contract called a *call option*.

To buy a call option you will start by making a few decisions:

1. At what price do you want the choice to buy the shares? (*strike price*)

2. How long do you want the option to last? (*expiration date*)

3. How much will the contract cost? (*option premium*)

KEY POINT!		
Three important parts of an option contract		
Strike Price	**Expiration Date**	**Premium**
The fixed price at which the stock shares can be bought or sold	**The date when the contract is no longer valid**	**The amount of money paid for the option contract**

So for this example, let's get the information we need:

1. Let's purchase a call-option contract that gives us the choice to buy this stock at $50.

2. Let's choose an option contract that expires in two months.

3. Let's say that this "layaway" cost—or option premium—is $3 per share.

Unlike the tailor who just wrote you an invoice, when you buy an option contract there is a small premium involved to give you the choice to purchase that stock at a set price. For our example, the premium here is $3 per share.

In the U.S. markets, a single option contract gives you control over 100 shares. Other world markets have option contracts that control up to 1,000 shares.

In our example, this means that instead of having to fork over $5,000 to own the stock, you will only have to risk $300 (100 shares at $3 per share) to buy a call option that controls $5,000 worth of stock (100 shares at $50 per share). This charge for the option contract is called the *premium,* which you pay to buy the call option. In this situation, your maximum risk is just the $300 you paid for the premium.

If the stock goes down, you are not obligated to buy it. Remember that "option" is another word for "choice."

Now let's look at what happens if that stock price shoots up from the original $50 to $100.

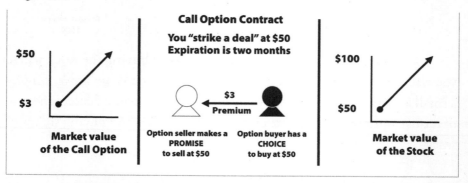

Agreement has $5,000 intrinsic value because you can buy 100 shares at $50 and then sell the 100 shares at $100 at the market.

Just as in the tuxedo scenario, you do not need to buy the shares any more than you needed to buy the tuxedo. Remember that you can sell the actual agreement all by itself. And because the options market is liquid, you can sell your call option contract at market value right from your computer with the click of a button.

If you sell the call option for $5,000 then your profit is $4,700 ($5,000 - $300) and your initial cash outlay and risk was only $300.

With this simple example, you can see there is a big difference between the large cash outlays required when you buy the stock itself and buying the options for that stock. With the option, you are *leveraging* a small amount of money. If we compare strategies of buying the stock versus buying the call option, this is what we get:

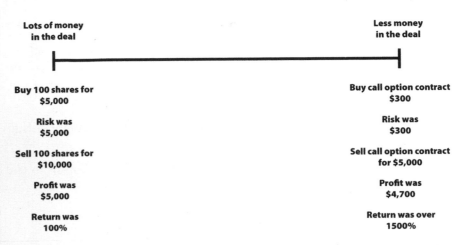

Strategy Comparison

Lots of money in the deal	Less money in the deal
Buy 100 shares for $5,000	**Buy call option contract** $300
Risk was $5,000	**Risk was** $300
Sell 100 shares for $10,000	**Sell call option contract for $5,000**
Profit was $5,000	**Profit was** $4,700
Return was 100%	**Return was over** 1500%

You can see there is quite a difference between buying the stock where you risk a lot of money and choosing the option where you are *leveraging* a small amount of money for large profits. And when we calculate the rate of return, options offer far greater potential returns than buying shares of stock.

Call Options and Expiry Date

Call options are dependent upon price and time. And it is the time element that carries much of the risk. If you hold that option until its expiration date without selling it or exercising it, it will be worth nothing. When it expires, you no longer have the right to buy the underlying stock at the predetermined price.

Since all options expire at some point, for the deal to work in your favor the underlying stock price must move in the direction you desire before expiration.

You might now be able to see more clearly why your ability to effectively position yourself rests on your skill with fundamental and technical analysis. Using these tools to see what is likely to happen (and when) is how you determine how to position yourself in the market. Of course, there is always an opportunity for an investor to look forward and buy whatever duration option is interesting.

To help investors keep track of all the different options available for a specific stock, there is a useful table called an *option chain.*

I remember when I took my first look at an option chain. It looked very complex, and I have to admit I was a little intimidated. But option chains are actually very easy to learn. The key is simply to know what you're looking for.

This particular option chain is for Microsoft (MSFT) and shows the call options that expired during Sept 2012.

MSFT (?)	Exp: Sep 2012 ⌄	Last	5 Day HV	20 Day HV	60 Day HV	90 Day HV	Continuous IV Calls
MICROSOFT CORP		29.64	20.50	24.25	24.50	23.00	20.75

Theta	Vega	Gamma	Delta	IV	OI	Volume	Net	Bid	Ask	Last	Symbol	Exp △
0.0000	0.0000	0.0000	0.0000	0.00	255	0	-1.20	6.60	6.65	6.30	O:MSF...	Sep12 23.00
0.0000	0.0000	0.0000	0.0000	0.00	167	5	0.20	5.60	5.70	5.60	O:MSF...	Sep12 24.00
0.0000	0.0000	0.0000	0.0000	0.00	884	20	0.03	4.60	4.70	4.80	O:MSF...	Sep12 25.00
-0.0011	0.0043	0.0203	0.9853	16.18	558	0	-0.25	3.65	3.70	3.15	O:MSF...	Sep12 26.00
-0.0034	0.0171	0.0735	0.9184	18.20	1336	17	-0.28	2.73	2.76	2.64	O:MSF...	Sep12 27.00
-0.0058	0.0311	0.1326	0.8051	18.42	3381	579	-0.17	1.89	1.91	1.83	O:MSF...	Sep12 28.00
-0.0076	0.0422	0.1817	0.6417	18.24	6108	337	-0.12	1.18	1.20	1.14	O:MSF...	Sep12 29.00
-0.0079	0.0447	0.1941	0.4496	18.09	17361	778	-0.08	0.66	0.67	0.66	O:MSF...	Sep12 30.00
-0.0067	0.0378	0.1620	0.2760	18.29	19162	488	-0.03	0.33	0.35	0.33	O:MSF...	Sep12 31.00
-0.0046	0.0262	0.1114	0.1484	18.42	16143	441	-0.02	0.15	0.16	0.16	O:MSF...	Sep12 32.00
-0.0030	0.0166	0.0674	0.0784	19.24	11325	205	-0.02	0.07	0.08	0.06	O:MSF...	Sep12 33.00

When looking to buy an option you need to consider three things:

1. *Strike price*: the price at which you want the choice to buy the shares of stock

2. *Expiration date:* the day the option expires

3. *Premium*: the amount of money the option seller is asking for the option contract

Let's look at the above option chain and find the information we need. First is the strike price. This part of the option chain helps us identify all of the different contracts that the option sellers are offering.

Sep12 23.00
Sep12 24.00
Sep12 25.00
Sep12 26.00
Sep12 27.00
Sep12 28.00
Sep12 29.00
Sep12 30.00
Sep12 31.00
Sep12 32.00
Sep12 33.00

You can see that on this option chain there are call options that will give you the choice to buy shares of MSFT (Microsoft) at a set price of $23 per share all the way up to $33 per share. Notice that next to the price you can see the date of Sep 12. This expiration date is selected by you. At the top of the option chain there are spaces to select what company stock options you want to see, the last price paid for the shares, and which expiration month you want to view.

We can see that the last trade on MSFT was $29.64.

Once you see a strike price you desire, you can see how much in premium the option seller is asking for the contract. Since MSFT is trading around $29, you can find out how much premium the option seller wants for a call option with a strike price of $29.

Bid	Ask	Last	Symbol	Exp	△
6.60	6.65	6.30	O:MSF...	Sep12 23.00	
5.60	5.70	5.60	O:MSF...	Sep12 24.00	
4.60	4.70	4.80	O:MSF...	Sep12 25.00	
3.65	3.70	3.15	O:MSF...	Sep12 26.00	
2.73	2.76	2.64	O:MSF...	Sep12 27.00	
1.89	1.91	1.83	O:MSF...	Sep12 28.00	
1.18	1.20	1.14	O:MSF...	Sep12 29.00	

On the option chain you can see that for a call option with a strike price of $29, the option seller is asking $1.20.

At any given time, you can select a given expiration month in an option chain and see the option contracts that will expire that month along with all the strike prices and premiums.

A *call option* provides an opportunity for profit when a stock price goes up because that gives you the choice to buy the stock at a set price no matter how high the share price may rise.

At the top we can see that the last price paid for shares of Microsoft stock is $29.64. That is the market price we would pay to buy the shares at that moment. But we are interested in buying an option on Microsoft.

As we go down the option chain table, notice that the call option contract with the **strike price** that is closest to the stock price on the day we were looking at the chain is highlighted. It's the Sep12 29.00 strike.

Theta	Vega	Gamma	Delta	IV	OI	Volume	Net	Bid	Ask	Last	Symbol	Exp
0.0000	0.0000	0.0000	0.0000	0.00	255	0	-1.20	6.60	6.65	6.30	O:MSF...	Sep12 23.00
0.0000	0.0000	0.0000	0.0000	0.00	167	5	0.20	5.60	5.70	5.60	O:MSF...	Sep12 24.00
0.0000	0.0000	0.0000	0.0000	0.00	884	20	0.03	4.60	4.70	4.80	O:MSF...	Sep12 25.00
-0.0011	0.0043	0.0203	0.9853	16.18	558	0	-0.25	3.65	3.70	3.15	O:MSF...	Sep12 26.00
-0.0034	0.0171	0.0735	0.9184	18.20	1336	17	-0.28	2.73	2.76	2.64	O:MSF...	Sep12 27.00
-0.0058	0.0311	0.1326	0.8051	18.42	3381	579	-0.17	1.89	1.91	1.83	O:MSF...	Sep12 28.00
-0.0076	0.0422	0.1817	0.6417	18.24	6108	337	-0.12	1.18	1.20	1.14	O:MSF...	Sep12 29.00
-0.0079	0.0447	0.1941	0.4496	18.09	17361	778	-0.08	0.66	0.67	0.66	O:MSF...	Sep12 30.00
-0.0067	0.0378	0.1620	0.2760	18.29	19162	488	-0.03	0.33	0.35	0.33	O:MSF...	Sep12 31.00
-0.0046	0.0262	0.1114	0.1484	18.42	16143	441	-0.02	0.15	0.16	0.16	O:MSF...	Sep12 32.00
-0.0030	0.0166	0.0674	0.0784	19.24	11325	205	-0.02	0.07	0.08	0.06	O:MSF...	Sep12 33.00

MSFT (?) Exp: Sep 2012 — Last: 29.64 — 5 Day HV: 20.50 — 20 Day HV: 24.25 — 60 Day HV: 24.50 — 90 Day HV: 23.00 — Continuous IV Calls: 20.75

MICROSOFT CORP

We can see that the **ask price** on that line is 1.20. This ask price is the **premium** you would invest for the choice to buy Microsoft at $29 any time between the time we took a picture of the option chain for our example and the expiration date in September of 2012.

Remember that each call option contract controls 100 shares of stock. In this example, you would buy this option for $120 ($1.20 x 100 shares). You would now have the option to buy 100 Microsoft shares for $29 per share at any time before expiration, no matter how high the share price might actually go during that time.

Based on your fundamental and technical analysis, you might have set a target price for Microsoft to hit $32 before it expires. The power of the option is that if you can buy 100 shares for $29 each, and the price goes up to $32 at expiration, your option would have $3 of intrinsic value for each of the 100 shares. The option you paid $1.20 to buy you can now sell on the open market for $3.

Remember the story of the real estate investors Mr. Cash and Mr. Credit? With a 10 percent move in the value of the asset, Mr. Cash gained a cash-on-cash return of 10 percent and Mr. Credit doubled his money. We could tell a similar story here with stock investors named Mr. Stock and Mr. Option. Except Mr. Option achieves his position of leverage with no debt.

Using a computer can make this very easy to see. Below is a risk graph that shows how much value your option will gain or lose as the price of MSFT moves.

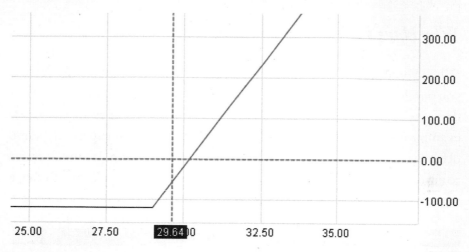

With this graph you can see that your maximum risk is a loss of $120. That makes sense because that is all you paid in premium for the call option contract. No matter how far MSFT might fall, you can't lose more than you put in. But the upside can be very exciting.

Own 100 Shares MSFT at $29/share

Maximum Risk $2,900

Own 1 MSFT 29 strike call option contract

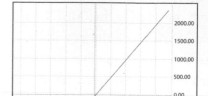

Maximum Risk $120

These graphs show the position of leverage achieved by reducing the amount of money you have in the investment. You can see that your profit soars by about $100 with each dollar MFST moves in price. In fact, your profit increases as if you already owned 100 shares of the stock because your option contract guarantees you can buy MSFT at $29 at any time during the term of the option. Also notice that this was a leveraged position achieved without going into debt. That is the power and leverage that's available with options.

Why Have I Been Told Options Are so Risky?

When you purchase shares of stock, you own shares of a company. When you purchase option contracts, you own agreements that have an expiration date. In order for you to lose 100 percent of your money in the stock example above, Microsoft would have to go bankrupt or experience some other event that would cause the share price to fall to zero. It's much easier to lose the money invested in your call option contract. Why? Because your option is comprised of time, and like an ice cube, it will melt away.

KEY POINT!

One difference between buying shares of stock and buying an option contract is OPTION CONTRACTS EXPIRE!

The risk here is that Microsoft shares will be trading below $30.20 ($29 + 1.20 premium) at the expiration date. If that happens, then your option will expire without sufficient intrinsic value. It's probably much more conceivable that MSFT will trade below $30.20 than the likelihood that MSFT stock shares will be trading at zero. On the one hand, you are much more likely to lose all your money invested in an option than in the stock, but on the other hand you can lose far more money by investing in one hundred shares of the stock than buying one option contract to control the same hundred shares. We will cover the really big lessons on how to manage the risk in both trades in the next chapter when we talk about exit strategies and other ways to mitigate risk.

For now, remember that part of the value of an option is that it buys you time for the stock to make its move. Discovering how time works in relation to option contracts is vital.

Time Value

Options have both intrinsic and time values. As time gets closer to the expiration date, the value of that time shrinks. To illustrate this important concept let's use another example.

You see a stock that looks promising, so you conduct a fundamental analysis and find the company to be financially strong and growing. Your technical analysis of the stock chart shows a strong bullish pattern. In fact, the stock has just broken out of an ascending triangle and is now trading at $52. How do you want to position yourself?

Strategy Comparison

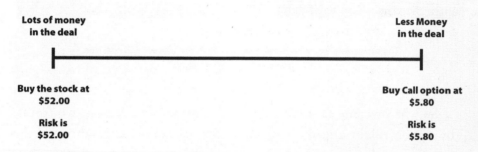

You begin by finding the three important pieces of information:

Strike Price: $50

Premium: $5.80

Time: Expires in 5 months

By choosing to buy the call option you achieve a position of leverage because you have put less money into the trade than if you bought the stock shares outright. And you still control the shares. Remember that you now have the choice to buy the stock at $50 anytime between now and the expiration date, which is five months out.

Since the stock is trading at $52 and you can buy at $50, your option has an intrinsic value of $2.

KEY POINT!

Intrinsic value for call options

If your strike price is lower than the stock price, then the call option has intrinsic value. The intrinsic value is the difference between the stock price and your option strike price.

It makes sense that if you can buy at $50 and then sell at the current price of $52, you would earn a profit of $2. That brings up an interesting question: If the call option has a value of just $2, why then did you have to pay a premium of $5.80? The reason is that you are also getting five months of time to decide what you want to do. Time is money and it has value.

KEY POINT!

Time is money.

The more time you want your option to last, the more it will cost you. This is known as "Time Value."

So when we buy an option we must consider its value on two fronts. The option might already have some intrinsic value, depending on the stock price and the strike price. Moreover, the option's time value depends on how much time is left before its expiration date.

You can determine the time value of an option very easily. In our example, the premium was $5.80. Let's figure out how much time value there is in this option.

Premium	Intrinsic value	Time value
$5.80	**$2.00**	**???**

In the chapter on fundamental analysis we concluded that price is what you pay and value is what you receive. If we pay $5.80 in premium and we know that $2 of what we paid was for the intrinsic value, then we know that the remaining $3.80 of the premium was for the five months in time value.

Premium $5.80	Intrinsic value $2.00	Time value $3.80

KEY POINT!

Option premium includes the option's intrinsic value and time value.
Time value + Intrinsic value = Premium

Time Decay

As the expiration date steadily creeps closer, the time value of the option will decrease, much like an ice cube melting in the sun. As a call-option buyer, you are anticipating a price move to the upside that will increase the intrinsic value of your option before time runs out.

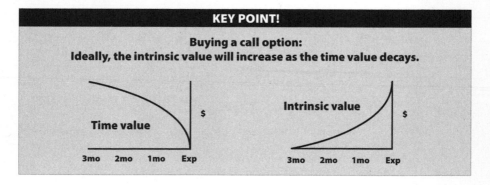

KEY POINT!

Buying a call option:
Ideally, the intrinsic value will increase as the time value decays.

Let's continue with our example and see how things play out with intrinsic value increasing as time value decays.

The technical analysis on the chart shows a slight ascending triangle, followed by a nice breakout to the upside. You have taken a position with a call option contract that allows you to buy the stock at $50 anytime over the next five months.

Premium	Time Value	Intrinsic Value	Stock Price	Strike Price
$5.80	**$3.80**	**$2.00**	**$52.00**	**$50.00**

A month passes and the stock is now standing at $61. You can still buy at $50, so the intrinsic value of the stock is now $11 per share. But there is less time before the expiration date, and the time value is therefore going to be lower. Notice that the value of the option reflects both the current intrinsic value of $11, and the reduced time value of $2.50, for a total premium of $13.50. Since the options market is liquid you could sell your option right now for a nice profit, but you still have plenty of time.

Premium	Time Value	Intrinsic Value	Stock Price	Strike Price
$13.50	**$2.50**	**$11.00**	**$61.00**	**$50.00**

Now let's move on. It's five months until the option is close to its expiry date. The stock is now trading at $71, which gives your call option an intrinsic value of $21, since you still have the choice to buy the stock shares at $50. Notice that now there is very little time value left. In fact there is only 60 cents left in time value, since the option is about to expire. It's time for you to *sell* your option.

Premium	Time Value	Intrinsic Value	Stock Price	Strike Price
$21.70	$0.60	$21.10	$71.10	$50.00

You can now *exchange* that option (which means the same as selling it) through the Options Exchange. You have the option to buy that stock at $50, but you don't want to actually hand over cash for the shares. Instead, you will now exchange that option electronically for its intrinsic value of $21.10 and time value of 60 cents. The final settlement price to exchange the option is $21.70.

Let's review what happened during this trade.

- In October, the stock was at $52.50.

- By February it was at $71.10.

- If you had purchased 1,000 shares of the stock, it would have cost you $52,500 and you could have sold your shares in February for $71,100.

- Your profit would have been $19,100—a 36 percent profit in five months.

Or...

- You could have bought 10 call-option contracts, since one contract controls 100 shares of stock. That would have given you the choice to buy 1,000 shares of stock at $50 any time over the next five months. The option premium was $5.80, costing you a total of $5,800.

- You then exchange (sell) the option and receive a premium of $21,700 for the intrinsic value plus the small amount of remaining time value.

- Subtract what you initially paid for the option and then work out the *rate of return:*

$$(\text{Money out} - \text{Money in}) \div \text{Money in}$$

$$(\$21,700 - \$5,800) \div \$5,800 = 274 \text{ percent return}$$

Paper Trading in a Virtual Account

As you learn more about trading options you can practice with *paper trading*, but don't think that this exercise does not take advantage of our high-tech world and its tools. The term might sound old school, but you trade using a *virtual account*. By paper trading in a virtual account you can practice your fundamental and technical analysis skills with no risk (zero, zilch, nada, none...) because virtual accounts do not use real money. The value of these trades comes through practicing on real stocks in real market situations. As you trade, try different strategies side-by-side and get a sense of the risk and reward for each.

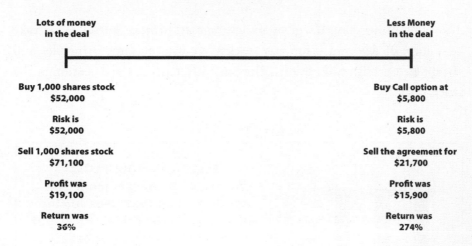

Strategy Comparison

Lots of money in the deal		Less Money in the deal
Buy 1,000 shares stock $52,000		Buy Call option at $5,800
Risk is $52,000		Risk is $5,800
Sell 1,000 shares stock $71,100		Sell the agreement for $21,700
Profit was $19,100		Profit was $15,900
Return was 36%		Return was 274%

After doing your homework using fundamental and technical analysis, you can look at an investing situation and choose to leverage your money with options to grow it more rapidly than most of the people who invest directly in stocks. The key is the leverage you gain with options. When used correctly, it can help you far exceed what most people consider possible with personal investments.

Opportunities to Make Money When the Market Falls

Every asset class has its own benefits. One of the great advantages of paper assets is the agility they offer investors in positioning themselves to benefit from markets whether they go up or down. When large problems in the fundamentals begin to appear and critical technical levels in the charts begin to break down, many investors want to protect their wealth and also grow it by exploiting moves to the downside. As you continue to study and gain a greater appreciation for fundamental analysis, technical analysis, positioning for cash flow, and risk management, you will also find that you will be less concerned about which direction the market is headed and more concerned about how you are positioned.

The Put Option

The put option contract gives us leverage to protect ourselves or take advantage of downward moving stocks. We use the same principles and vocabulary as with call options. The only difference is the direction of the stock price.

BUILD ON IT

PILLAR #3: CASHFLOW
An option is an agreement with another trader that gives you the right to buy (call option) or sell (put option) a certain stock at a pre-determined price.

Let's go through a simple example of a put option. Suppose you're looking at a stock that is currently trading at $100, and your fundamental and technical analysis leads you to think it will likely trend down for a few months.

The traditional way for an investor to take action in this situation is to short the stock. You could take a short position by borrowing 100 shares from the brokerage now and selling them for $100 each, giving you a total of $10,000. Sure enough, the company hits hard times just as the fundamentals suggested and the share price drops to $50. You can then buy your shares back for $5,000 and return the borrowed shares to the broker. Your profit is the difference between the price you sold the shares at and the price at which you subsequently bought back the shares: $5,000. But your risk was theoretically infinite since the shares could have shot right up through the ceiling. You would, of course, have had an exit strategy to prevent this, but on paper this is still an infinite risk. Is there another way to position yourself to profit from the downside and limit the risk? Yes—you could buy a *put option*.

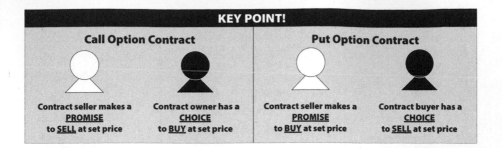

Let say you buy a *put option* at a strike price of $100 and a premium of $3. In essence, this gives you the choice to sell 100 shares at the set price of $100 anytime between now and the expiration date. Just like a call option, you don't need to own the stock. You just need to control the ability to sell it at a higher price.

So you take action and buy a put option on the stock. You now have the option to sell the stock at $100 per share. You have bought this option for a premium of $3 per share, which means you paid $300 for the option, and that is the only amount you risk losing. When the shares drop to $50, you buy 100 shares for a total of $5,000 and sell them with your option for the market price of $10,000.

Agreement has $5,000 intrinsic value because you
can buy 100 shares at $50 and then sell the 100 shares at $100 at the market.

You have made $5,000, less the cost of the premium of $300. Your reward is $4,700, and your risk was only $300.

As mentioned in Chapter Two, all asset classes have their own vocabulary. Part of your financial education is to become more familiar and fluent with the language of money. In this chapter on positioning we introduced many new words that are now part of your financial lexicon.

Vocabulary Review

Call Option—After doing your fundamental and technical analysis, if you think a stock is likely to go up in value, you can buy a *call option* to gain more leverage. The call option means that you have a guaranteed opportunity to buy that stock at a set price called the *strike price*.

Put Option—If you think a stock is likely to drop, you can buy a *put option* for leverage. It gives you a chance to sell the stock at the *strike price*.

Strike Price—The purchase price of the stock agreed by the parties of the option agreement. A *call option* allows the owner of the option to buy the stock at that agreed price at any time before the *expiration date* for the option.

Premium—In order to buy an option, the buyer of the option agreement will pay the seller some money for the option. This is called a *premium*.

Option Chain—A table that includes all the essential information we need in order to make a choice on whether or not to enter into an option, including the *expiration date*, the *strike price* and the *premium*.

Intrinsic Value—The difference between the *strike price* and the actual value of the share price.

Time Value—The option premium less any intrinsic value.

Rate of Return—You can calculate your *rate of return* on any trade with a simple formula where V_f stands for Final Value and V_i stands for Initial Value: $(V_f - V_i) \div V_i$. You can then multiply this return by 100 to get your percentage return.

Remember to give yourself permission to learn new terms at your own pace, to review things more than once, and use the help of mentors to supplement your reading. Take the opportunity to solidify what you are learning by sharing it with others.

Once you know the basics of call and put options, you are ready to begin exploring how you can use these investment tools to generate a steady cash flow.

Getting an Income

Cash flow is about positioning. We want to make money if the market goes down; we want to make money if the market goes up; we want to make money if the market goes sideways.

There is no bad news in the market. There is only positioning. That's a big idea to get your head around, I know. But let me make it simple: If gas goes up to $16 a gallon, is that good or bad? If you're buying gas, it's probably bad news. But if you're selling gas, it's probably good news. The value is in the eye of the beholder, and that is based on position. Is your position that of the buyer or the seller? You can't control the market, but you can control your position. See the power?

Buy-and-hold investing, such as what you typically see with mutual funds and 401(k) plans, is usually an attempt to increase the value of an entire account through capital gains. When the market goes up, the account goes up. When the market goes down, the account goes down. That is not cash flow investing. Cash flow investing should offer:

- Proven strategies to extract cash from the market on one's own timetable

- Ability to make profits at regular intervals

- Excellent rates of return

- Ways to manage the risk to protect capital

- Simple enough stategies for the average person to learn and implement on his or her own

Options and Time Decay

As we learned about the basics of options, we saw that one of the most important factors to consider was the amount of time until the option's expiration date. As each minute passes between now and that expiration date, the total amount of time steadily diminishes until it ultimately reaches zero. As you will recall, this movement of time during the option's life is called *time decay*.

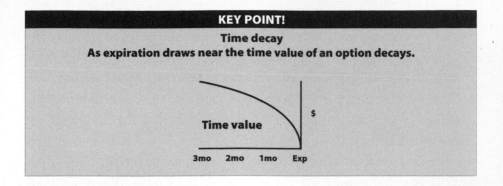

KEY POINT!

Time decay
As expiration draws near the time value of an option decays.

Time value $

3mo   2mo   1mo   Exp

Educated investors already know that time decay is an excellent opportunity to generate cash.

Real estate investors know that investment cash flow relies heavily on time decay. In the chapter on fundamental analysis we learned that by looking at financial statements we could determine the strength of an entity. Just as an option agreement has two parties, so does the rental or lease agreement. You can evaluate the financial statement for each of the two parties. In doing so you can determine which of the two parties is most likely to become rich.

Let's look at the financial statements of each party to a common lease agreement and make some observations:

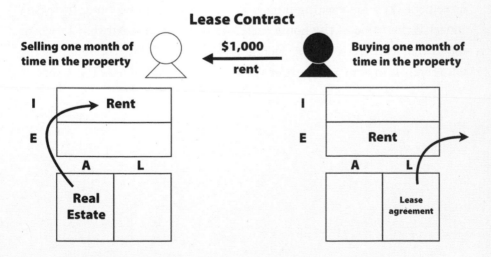

Lease Contract

Selling one month of time in the property — $1,000 rent — Buying one month of time in the property

Let's suppose that you are a landlord who owns a house. I need to find a place to live, and your house looks very nice. You agree to lease me the house in exchange for regular monthly rent payments. For me, our lease agreement is a liability because I must pay you a monthly rent amount. On my income statement, it is shown as an expense, since money flows out of my account. I am not buying the house from you, I'm simply buying time. When I give you the rent check, you agree to allow me to live there for a certain amount of time. At the beginning of the month I might pay $1,000. But that money only buys me a month of time. When that time expires, I have nothing left.

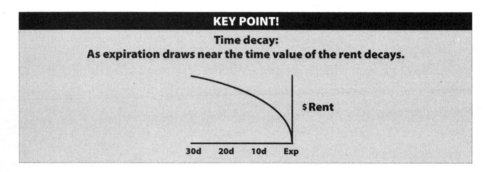

KEY POINT!

Time decay:
As expiration draws near the time value of the rent decays.

$ Rent

30d   20d   10d   Exp

On the other hand, you are now receiving income because of the lease agreement. You are earning money on the movement of time. It doesn't matter if the value of the house increases or decreases. All that concerns you is that you are receiving income. With time decay, the seller of the lease receives income independent of the underlying value of the asset.

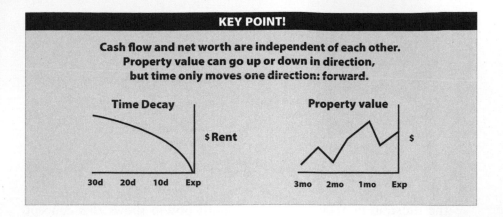

With options, the time decay is somewhat similar to this example. Just like a lease agreement, options have expiration dates. When you buy an option for three months, the premium (think of it as *time value*) is at its highest due to the large amount of time remaining until expiration. The premium is lower for a two-month option because there is less time available to buy. For a one-month option, the premium is even lower because the time is quickly running out.

You can see time decay has the look of an exponential graph rather than a linear graph. More simply stated, you can see here that the closer an option gets to its expiration date, the faster it loses time value. When buying an option, an investor typically wants plenty of time remaining. This allows the intrinsic value to increase as the time value diminishes. As a general rule of thumb, I usually want two months or more until expiration so that there is plenty of time for that intrinsic value to rise.

However, when it's time to sell an option, I typically want to sell it closer to expiration and book my profits because there is not as much time for the intrinsic value to increase much more, and the time value decay is much faster.

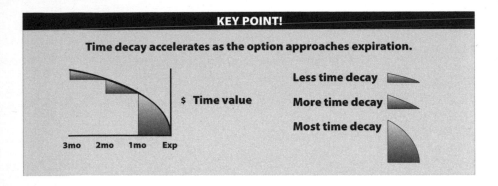

The illustration above of a three-month option shows this concept very clearly. From three months remaining to two months remaining, we lose very little value due to time decay. From two months to one month, a bit more of the value is whittled away. But look at what happens in the last month, also called the *front month,* when the option expires. The option rapidly loses all its value through time decay as that expiration approaches.

Frequently, naïve option investors make a critical mistake I want to help you avoid. When they look at an option premium during the front month, they often see how inexpensive it is and think it's a good time to buy. As I explained before, the closer you get to expiration, the less time there is for the intrinsic value to increase. Which means you are flirting with the risk of having your option expire worthless because it didn't increase in value for you.

One of the things that makes options different from stocks is that options expire. So you must not forget the importance of time when you take a position of leverage. The following example looks good on paper, but this leveraged position does not give the investor much time.

The last price for ACME is $250 per share. An investor looking at this stock realizes that to buy one thousand shares of ACME would require $250,000. Then that investor looks at the option chain and sees that a call option is just $5 a share. By comparison, the investor can control the same 1,000 shares of stock for just $5,000 of option premium.

Strategy Comparison

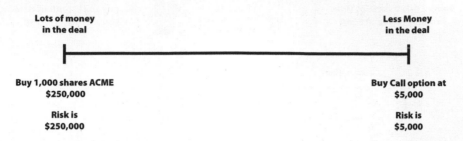

On the surface, this looks like a very attractive investment opportunity. The difference is, of course, that when you buy the stock directly there is no time limit on how long you can hold that stock as you wait for it to gain in value. With the option, that expiration date is very near. Given such a limited amount of time, it's difficult to imagine that the underlying stock price will rise enough to give you a good return on your investment. Moreover, if the stock were to fall even slightly, then the option would expire worthless and all of the premium would be lost.

Strategy Comparison

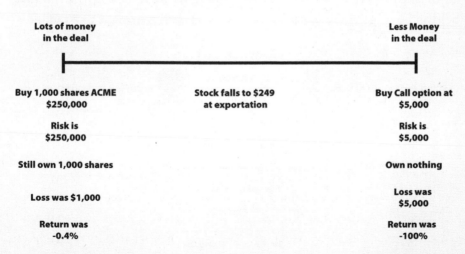

In this case, the seller of the option came out with a great profit and the buyer was the loser.

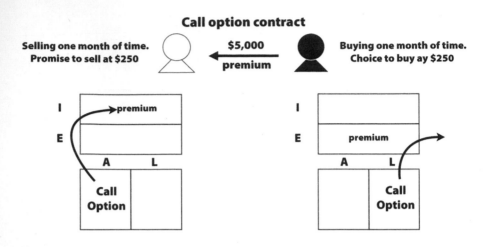

Call option contract

Selling one month of time.
Promise to sell at $250

$5,000
premium

Buying one month of time.
Choice to buy ay $250

Cash Flow vs Speculation

Let's revisit the situation with real estate investing to help us get a clear picture of how you might find cash flow investing more suitable to you than mere speculation that the value of the overall investment will increase over an extended period of time. For this example, we'll look at the numbers behind buying a house with a mortgage and then renting it to a tenant.

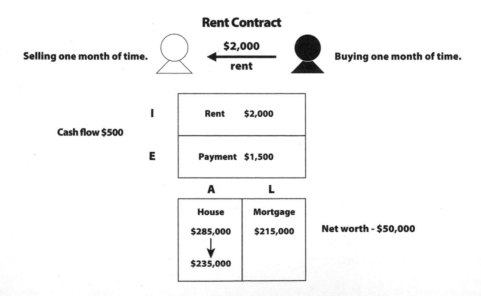

Rent Contract

Selling one month of time.

$2,000
rent

Buying one month of time.

Cash flow $500

| I | Rent | $2,000 |
| E | Payment | $1,500 |

A	L
House	Mortgage
$285,000	$215,000
$235,000	

Net worth - $50,000

You originally bought this house for $285,000 and took out a mortgage for $215,000. Your mortgage repayment is $1,500 a month. The tenant in your property is paying you rent of $2,000 a month, giving you a positive cash flow of $500 per month.

Of course, the actual market value of your house can go up or down depending on economic conditions. For this scenario, suppose that the recent negative economy causes the value of your house to drop to $235,000. Instantly, your home has decreased in value by $50,000 because of market conditions beyond your control. However, you are still obligated to pay the $1,500 monthly mortgage payment. Likewise, your tenant still pays you $2,000 per month for rent. And you still have positive monthly cash flow of $500. No matter what happens with the value of the house, you are still entitled to the rent. The deposits to your bank account from collecting rent will continue regardless of the price fluctuations of your rental property.

This is a chart of the 2008 IYR, the Dow Jones Real Estate Index. On the top it shows how the value of real estate dropped with the meltdown in 2008. Virtually all real estate lost value during this time period.

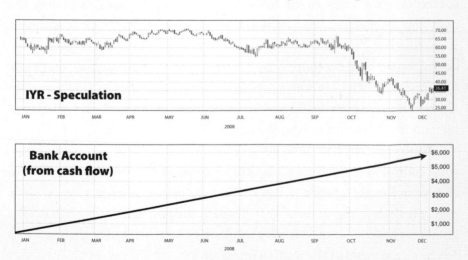

By comparison, the bottom half of the chart shows how during the same time period a positive cash flow of $500 from your real estate income totals $6,000 in that year. This is a prime example of a really good investment: even though the underlying value sunk, your wealth continued to rise through cash flow. This is the sign of a true investor —when he or she is still making bank deposits from positive cash flow—even when the underlying asset decreases in value.

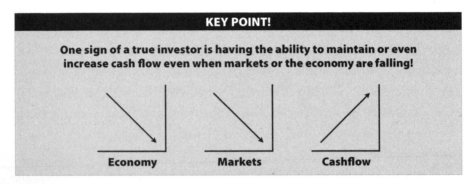

KEY POINT!

One sign of a true investor is having the ability to maintain or even increase cash flow even when markets or the economy are falling!

Economy   **Markets**   **Cashflow**

This points to a very important concept for investors. There are sometimes two sides to an investment: the capital-gain side, and the cash-flow side. As we have shown, the capital gain side of an investment is speculative. You have no control over whether the market goes up or down, so you have no control over the value of the investment. That's one of the reasons why I'm not convinced mutual funds or 401(k) plans are always all they're cracked up to be—you have no control over what will happen to the market during the time of your investment.

With the cash flow side, however, we've shown that you have almost total control over the time decay. The example of the rental house showed that you can deposit substantial amounts of money in your account from rent, even while the value of that house is dropping. This is what I call a good investment, because it pays you money no matter how the market is affecting the value of the underlying asset.

Cash Flow from Selling a Covered Call Option

Now let's shift from real estate examples into actual ways we can use this cash-flow strategy to make real money with options in the markets. This is especially useful in difficult markets where buy-and-hold investors are suffering from crazy up and down conditions.

As a quick reminder, an option is a promise by someone to sell a certain stock at an agreed-upon price until a certain date. In return for this promise, he receives a premium as income. This premium is not just based on the movement of the stock price, but on the movement of time.

As a teacher, I've seen how hard it is for many people to grasp the ideas of time decay and cash flow in the stock market. I know it certainly took some time for the light to come on for me. So a few years ago I made a small trade just for the purpose of teaching. I chose to hold a stock for a long time regardless of the fluctuation in its value, just as real many estate investors hold their rental property regardless of fluctuations in the price.

To show my students the similarities between stock investors selling options and real estate investors collecting rent, I bought an ETF and held it for a year. It's not my usual practice to hold stocks that long, let alone buy anything that is heading down. But my goal was to prove that it is possible for a falling stock to generate income just as a house that is declining in value can still generate rent. This is not hypothetical. This is an actual series of very small trades I did during the subprime meltdown of 2008.

My first step was to buy 500 shares of an exchange-traded fund called the Spyder Trust (SPY), which mimics the S&P 500. I was going to hold it for a year, come what may. After buying it, I watched it closely to see if it going up, down, or sideways.

Since I owned the shares, I was positioned to be the seller of an option instead of the option buyer. (If you think back to our earlier example, it was as if I were the tailor who was selling the option to layaway the $1,000 tuxedo.)

After buying 500 shares of SPY, I then sold five one-month call option contracts on the SPY at a premium of $2.15. I promised the buyer that he could buy the Spy for $154 (which was more than I paid for the SPY) at any time before the expiration date.

The stock could now go in one of three directions.

- If the stock went up and he wanted to buy at $154, I would have made money since I bought it at a lower price.

- If the stock went sideways and stayed below $154, the option would expire worthless, and I would have kept my $2.15 (multiplied by 500) premium in cash flow. This is just like a house where the value remains the same. I would still be getting that rent as income.

- If the stock went down, the option would expire worthless, and I would keep my $2.15 premium (multiplied by 500).

You can see that I have set up a scenario where no matter what happened, I would generate income from an asset I had purchased. To me, this was a very attractive way to generate my own income. I bought 500 shares and then I sold those options. That's five one-month contracts of 100 shares, each at a premium of $2.15. When you do the math, you'll see that I created an income of $1,075, less the brokerage fee, so I received a net $1,061.

Even though the stock was falling in value, I continued to sell options on my shares of the SPY month in and month out for a whole year. Why? Because I am not much different than a real estate investor who sees the value of his rental house decline for a season. He is receiving his rent each month and I am also receiving my income every month from options. This income flows in even as we both wait for the underlying value of the assets to bounce back. I get to keep the stock while the time decay is bringing in cash.

This shows you how simple it can be to own stock assets and generate an income from them.

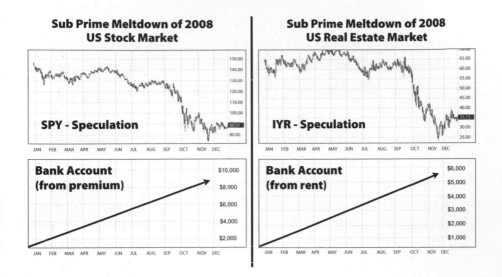

True cash flow investing is when the underlying asset, whether it's a house or stock, can go down but cash flow stays fairly consistent.

Covered Options

You may have noticed that I talked previously about a *covered call option*. This is another new term for you to learn. When I sold those 5 call options on the SPY, I promised the buyers that they could buy the shares from me for $154. If the buyers wanted to buy the shares, I owned the shares and would have been able to sell them. That is, I would have been able to deliver in the case of a call option because I actually owned the shares. I was *covered* by the stock I owned. I could keep my promise.

Let's suppose that I want to sell a put option. I promise the buyer of this put option that he can sell stock to me at the strike price. I have to be able to deliver in this case, which I do by having cash in the trade account. I am *covered* in the case of a put option by having enough cash there to buy the stock as I promised.

When selling options, either call options or put options, it's important to be *covered* so that you can deliver. You don't want to approach any of these strategies *naked*—which is the technical term for not possessing the cash or underlying stock to deliver when needed. Selling options naked is a very aggressive strategy and only for the most advanced traders. As a foundation strategy, we should keep all the trades small, keep them very controlled, and keep them covered.

How Warren Buffett Generates Huge Profits with Options

If you follow the world of investing at all, you are probably familiar with the famous investor Warren Buffett. Buffett sells a lot of options. Why? Because he understands how time decay works to the benefit of the option seller. Options provide him with a great tool to generate additional income for his holding company.

As you know, a put option has a time value and an expiration date. The person who buys the put option has the option of selling something at an agreed upon price before an expiration date. This put option is like an insurance policy. For example, if you own a stock that's at $100 and you buy a put option to sell it at $100 and it drops to zero, you're insured. The guy who sold you the option has to buy that stock at $100.

Put options can also be a very useful way to buy something you want. Here's how it works: when you sell a put option, you are making a promise to buy the stock at a certain price before expiration. It is important to remember this key point from the last chapter:

So rather than just buying a stock, you can earn extra cash by promising to buy the stock. This is a method Warren Buffett has used for years.

Let's pretend that Warren Buffett wants to increase his holdings in Coca-Cola (KO).

Let's say that Coca-Cola stock is trading at $39 per share. Buffett conducts a fundamental analysis and has decided that he is willing to buy at $35. Let's say he sells 5 million put options with a $35 strike price for a premium of $1.50. That would be an income of $7.5 million. Now let's look at three outcome possibilities: up, down and sideways. If Coke shares fell below $35, the option buyer would then *sell* their shares to Buffett and he would keep his promise to buy at $35. Remember that $35 was the price he wanted anyway! If the share price of Coke climbed instead, Buffett would still be happy with the fact that he collected a $1.50 option premium ($7.5 million). And of course the same would be true if the stock held steady at $39.

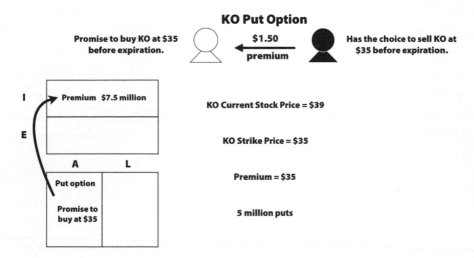

KO Put Option

Let's dissect this story in terms of what we have learned about investing so far:

In investing circles, Buffett is known as a fundamental anaylst. After doing this basic analysis, perhaps he thinks, "At $39 the stock is a little steep, but I would be interested if it got down to $35." Based on his own criteria, he sets a target at $35 at which point he is willing to buy that stock.

Instead of just waiting to see what will happen, Buffett decides to profit from the situation. So he writes (sells) 5 million put options. What this means is that Warren Buffett has made a promise to buy 5 million shares from the people or person who has purchased this contact from him.

For this trade, Buffett has a $35 strike price with a premium of $1.50. This means he has promised to buy the shares at a price of $35 to the investors who pay him a premium of $1.50 per share.

Most people have no idea what this story means. But with the brief education you have received so far in this book, you can fully understand what Buffett is doing and you can appreciate the strategy he has employed to make a profit no matter what happens to the actual price of Coke.

You might be wondering why anyone would buy the put option to sell the shares at $35. For investors who currently own the shares, they are looking at these options as an insurance opportunity. Perhaps they own the shares, and they are aware there is a possibility that the shares may go down. That's why they might be willing to pay a premium in order to have the option of selling those shares at $35 to mitigate any situation where the stock might suddenly drop even lower. They may have originally bought the shares for under $35, so they might be quite happy to have that insured as their selling price if the shares go down, in order to lock in their profit.

In this scenario, the following could happen:

Share Price Drops—The shares could go down to $35 or below and the people who bought the put options could "put" or sell their shares to Buffett. Buffett would be forced to buy 5 million shares because he made a promise to buy there. But this wouldn't worry him. If the shares had been at $35 today, he would have bought them. He believes $35 is a good value. If the price then went down below $35, it wouldn't bother him because he's often investing for the long term. He was willing to take the risk of holding the shares anyway if the price goes down.

Share Price Rises—If the shares rise, it wouldn't bother him either because he isn't interested in them at a valuation above $35. But he would be happy enough because he would collect $7.5 million in premium, just to watch it advance higher than the $35 he was prepared to spend.

Share Price Stays the Same—Similar to the 'price rises' scenario, Buffett isn't interested in anything above $35. But he would still pocket the $7.5 million in premiums.

KEY POINT!
Educated investors position themselves in such a way that they can be happy regardless of what direction the market goes.

No matter what happens, Buffett will receive the premium from this trade. This is a cash-flow strategy that Buffett and other educated investors use all the time, not just with stocks but with other derivatives as well. It's a sharp contrast to the average, less-educated 401(k) investor.

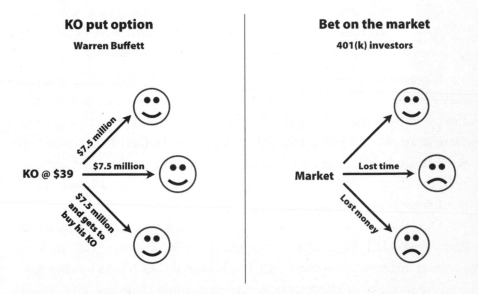

As I mentioned, Buffett has collected a premium from options as a means to generate income for a long time. He gets paid to make promises. In his car insurance business he collects premiums from people who accept his promises to pay for damages if something bad happens to their cars. But selling put options at a strike price lower than today's stock price means he gets paid upfront for making a promise to buy things that he wants to buy anyway. And by structuring deals intelligently, he also gets to buy what he wants later at a lower price than what it's selling for today. And by selling calls with a strike price that is higher than today's price, he gets paid to sell something he wants to sell anyway at a higher price than today's price.

Karen Richardson of the *Wall Street Journal* highlighted the magnitude of Buffett's income from premiums in a story titled "Buffett Scores with Derivatives." In that article, she said:

> *Billionaire insurance salesman Warren Buffett has been selling more derivatives recently.*
>
> *This year, Berkshire Hathaway Incorporated, the Omaha, Nebraska holding company headed by Mr. Buffett, has collected premiums of about $2.5 billion from selling insurance on stock indexes and bonds in the form of derivative contracts which guarantee payment to the buyer in the event of a specific loss in an underlying entity of the contracts.*

It's easy to be impressed by these large numbers. Perhaps some investors may even be intimidated and think that only big players such as Buffett can profit from these strategies. But smaller investors can easily use these same strategies in more scaled-down situations. In fact, I have used this same strategy of selling options to acquire certain stocks that I want to hold for a long time. All it takes is an understanding of how it works and if it fits your investing strategy.

One example of how I use this in my own positioning is with an exchange-traded fund that tracks the price of commodities such as precious metals such as silver (SLV)) and corn (CORN). As an educator, I refuse to make predictions or recommendations. I do not give people financial advice. I will say that I am very concerned with the sovereign fundamentals around the world, as well as the fiscal and monetary policies that shape them.

As a result, in my own holdings I like the idea of hedging against any devaluing of the dollar and I like to receive income by selling put options that allow me to buy exchange-traded funds that track commodities. I own some gold as a hedge, and also some exchange-traded funds that mimic precious metals. There are many people who debate over which is better: bullion or ETFs. In my opinion, making a blanket statement that one is better than the other is a mistake. Why? Because every investor's situation is different. One of the reasons I like the idea of taking a position in an ETF that tracks commodities is that I can acquire ownership of the ETF using the same strategies we discussed in the Warren Buffett example above.

Let's say that I would like to own some shares of SLV and I want to hold them long term as a hedge against the U.S. dollar. Rather than just going out and purchasing the shares, I could sell put options at a strike price that is slightly lower than the current price of the ETF today. By doing so, I place myself in a position similar to Warren Buffett's in the example we just covered.

SLV put option

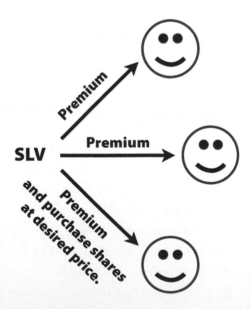

If the price of SLV goes up before expiration, I'm happy to get paid for watching it go there. It's true that if I purchased SLV and it goes up I might have received a large capital gain, but that is beyond my control. I really can't determine, exactly, where it may or might not go—even with the best technical analysis tools. In essence, I am happy with a bird in the hand rather than going for two in the bush, knowing that I can collect the premium upfront immediately.

To review:

- If the price of SLV remains the same, I'm just as happy to get paid for watching it stay there.

- If the price of SLV goes down below the strike price of my option, I'll be purchasing my shares of SLV at the price I determined at the outset of the agreement. It's true that I might be purchasing my shares at a higher price than the market price of SLV at expiration. But the reality is that if I just bought the stock directly, that's a risk I was going to take anyway. Since I believe that SLV will rise in the long-term based on sovereign fundamentals, it's really no more downside risk than I would have been exposed to had I simply bought the shares initially.

- So I'm likely to be quite happy with what SLV does during the course of the option contract. You can see why selling put options is one of my favorite ways to generate income.

In all of these cases I'm free to sell options on the SLV again the following month. If SLV remains the same or goes up, the options will expire worthless and I will keep the premium. That leaves me free with cash that can cover the promises I will make with new put contracts for the next month. If the stock goes down and the stock is assigned to me, I can sell covered call options on the ETF to generate income should I choose to sell SLV at a higher price later on.

It's quite common that investors can get 2 to 3 percent return on their money for selling one month put options. For example, if you have $50,000 sitting in a bank account, you would be fortunate to earn much interest these days. By holding your money in cash, your main risk is that the value of your cash will go down. However, if you're willing to convert that $50,000 into silver (SLV shares) at a set price, then you could receive a premium of say $1,000 for a put option. That's a 2 percent return in a month, and your main risk is that the price of silver will go down. How would you feel if your employer were to say that the company policy was going to change and he was going to pay you in silver instead of in dollars? It's an interesting thing to think about.

I want to reiterate that I'm not suggesting people go out and buy silver or gold. Your financial statement is probably different than mine, and your goals, age, and tolerance for risk might be different. You might have more or less financial education than I do as well.

When it comes to collecting premiums, the essence of the lesson on covered calls and cash covered puts is you can get paid to buy the things you want to buy, and you can get paid to sell the things you want to sell.

Collecting premiums from selling calls or puts is a primary way to generate income using time decay. As you continue along the Education Continuum, you will discover that there are many ways to position yourself to collect premiums from selling options in the stock market.

The important thing here is to realize that you don't have to be Warren Buffett to take advantage of strategies that allow you to collect premiums for cash flow. You can use the same strategies he uses because the same educational opportunities are open to you.

Constant Ongoing Source for Income

There are many people who wish they could own a business, but have struggled to come up with a product to sell. In addition, they haven't received the proper education or experience to run a large business well. Others dream of being a large real estate investor but haven't yet learned how to raise capital and do not yet have sufficient real estate education to get involved without getting themselves into trouble.

I love learning more about all of the asset classes. But what sticks out in my mind in relationship to the stocks and options market is the exciting concept that there is always an opportunity to collect premiums month in and month out.

I realized very quickly that the stock and options markets were liquid and that there are always buyers and sellers every single month, year in and year out. One of the reasons I want to get better and better at selling options is because this is an ongoing income opportunity that anyone can tap into after receiving some education.

My biggest hope at this point in this book is that you've come to the realization that there is such a thing as stock market cash flow. I hope that you realize that you don't have to ride the ups and downs of the stock market as a mutual fund investor in order to be a participant in the market.

When most people first learn about options they usually get very excited. And rightly so. Buying and selling options *is* exciting. But be careful. This is the point at which a little education can be dangerous. Option premium is also influenced by volatility in addition to time decay and changes in the stock price. And education in these areas and how they work is vital. Earning cash flow with options is for investors who first want to educate themselves.

This book is written for the beginner investor and is designed to help as they progress along the Education Continuum™. I highly recommend that you refer to the Education Continuum™ often as you study any topic—especially investing. That's because in everyone's financial education are points where people learn just enough to be dangerous. You've probably hit that point here.

KEY POINT!

Everyone has certain points in their financial education where they have learned just enough to be dangerous.

Learning to develop streams of income from stock market cash flow can give you huge benefits because most of these techniques are free from the boilerplate investment advice doled out by the mutual fund and the 401(k) industries. Please don't think that this is an easy path that can be taken casually. Quite the contrary: No matter what investment class you may invest in, it is an environment where many people fail. When I've failed, it's usually been because of my own ignorance or arrogance or lack of discipline to follow the rules. The more time I spend on my journey as a serious student, the more convinced I am that I want to continue to learn and that more education will always pay off.

These chapters have helped you move along the Education Continuum by improving your awareness of how cash flow can be generated from basic option trades. Now we're ready to look, in more depth, at what kinds of risks we face as cash flow investors and how to manage those risks to protect ourselves as much as possible. Because no matter how smart you may be as an investor, if you cannot effectively manage and even eliminate your risk, then you can get yourself into big trouble.

Risk management is about taking control of your investing. As you learn how to take control, you will be in a position to maximize your cash flow and returns.

Chapter Summary

Let's review some of the important points of Chapter Six:

1. Fundamental and technical analysis helps you in the first phase of investing to gain more information. Cash flow and risk management strategies help you in the second phase where you will determine how to position yourself in the market.

   By learning different positioning strategies, you are no longer required to hope for bull markets all the time.

2. An investment in the stock or options market can serve any one or more of three purposes: a capital gain, cash flow, or protection of your assets with a hedge.

3. Rate of return is (money out – money in) / (money in).

4. Infinite return is achieved when an investor receives a return from an investment that requires none of his own money be invested in the deal.

5. There are two ways to go for bigger returns: try to get lucky and find a ten bagger or reduce your initial investment.

6. An option contract is an agreement where one party has a choice and the other party makes a promise.

   Another word for the word *choice* is *option*. Options are a way to take control of the stock without having to purchase the stock.

7. Some options have *intrinsic value*.

   Intrinsic value is the difference between the price at which you can buy or sell, and what the market will pay for shares of that stock.

8. Three important parts of an option contract are the *strike price*, the *expiration date*, and the *option premium*.

   The strike price is the fixed price agreed upon in the option contract for which the stock shares can be bought or sold. The expiration date is the date on which the contract is no longer valid. The premium is the amount of money that is paid for an option contract.

9. One difference between buying shares of stock and buying an option contract is that the option contract expires.

   Many investors consider options to be more risky because it is certain that they will expire and, at that point, become worthless. Some investors might feel good about holding stock when the price goes down because there's always a chance the stock will go back up as long as the company doesn't go bankrupt. However, with an option contract the stock must go in the desired direction before its expiration date to become valuable.

10. Time is money. The more time you want before your option expires, the more it will cost you. This is known as *time value*.

    There are many factors that go into determining time value of an option, including the volatility of the stock, interest rates, the distance of the option's strike price from the current price of the stock, as well the amount of time in the option before expiration.

11. Option premium includes the option's intrinsic value and time value. An investor who is purchasing an option should identify how much of the premium is intrinsic value and how much of the premium is time value. As expiration draws near, the time value of an option decays.

12. With a call option contract, the buyer of the option has the choice to buy at the strike price and the seller of the option makes a promise to sell the stock at the strike price. With a put option, the contract buyer of the option has the choice to sell the stock at the strike price and the seller of the option makes a promise to buy the stock at the strike price.

    Understanding both call options and put options is the beginning of expanding the many different ways an investor can position himself or herself in the market.

Chapter Seven

Pillar 4: Risk Management

Basic risk management is the fourth, final, and most important of the Four Pillars. Have you ever heard of the World Championship of Trading? It's an annual competition where traders from around the world test their skills against each other and the market. Many of them enter the competition with fancy computer programs and all sorts of strategies to earn huge profits and take home the title. Typically, though, it's not these high-flying futures traders that win the trophy. Instead, it's the traders who know how to manage risk. It is the traders that know how to avoid a large loss—versus those that try to go for big gains.

Because I speak to so many groups of investors, I inevitably meet a lot of people who like to toot their own horns about their stock-picking skills: "I bought this stock and it went sky high." I just smile and congratulate them, even though what they are telling me may be no different than the person who had a lucky night at the tables in Vegas. Anyone can get lucky and have a stock shoot up to make some profits. But a few fortunate picks doesn't make them an all-star investor.

What impresses me is the investor who can say, "I was in this investment and the thing tanked, and this is how I minimized my losses." Why is this a better position as an investor? Because minimizing losses proves that you are in control of your investment. You aren't just hoping and praying for the best. You have actively taken actions that put you in control of the situation.

If you buy a stock and *hope* it will go up, you are out of control. That's why investors who have their life savings in 401(k) plans and mutual funds have virtually no control of their future. They believe the financial industry's sales pitch about the safety of their money, but the truth is they are just hoping and praying that the market will go higher so they can survive in retirement. No wonder so many people are so stressed out all the time. I don't like having something as important as my financial future out of my control.

Now that we have discussed some of the basics of analyzing a possible investment and how to position for generating cash flow, let's look at some powerful ways to manage our risk. For any type of investor, keeping a tight leash on risk is perhaps the most important skill you can have.

By studying more about the Risk Management Pillar, you will:

- Learn how to identify several kinds of common risk

- Understand the truth about risk and control

- Discover some powerful risk management techniques

- See when investment diversification can actually be dangerous

- Uncover the vital link between risk and education

- Learn how you can actually enter an order in the market that will minimize your risk

When we decide to put our money in the stock market, there is one rule we should remember: Always **expect the unexpected**.

That's why we should take the time to learn about the different potential risks we might face when we put our money into an investment. There are many different risks we need to manage. Most people have no idea how risky it can be in the market. If they don't know how to identify and neutralize those risks, it might be just a matter of time until they get pummeled by them.

One of the activities I am involved with is working as a Boy Scout leader. Other Scout leaders and I take the scouts to the shooting range and show them how to manage risk, and sometimes we will show them how to shoot a firearm. How do we manage the risk? **Massive, intense, unbreakable rules**. If there were ever an accident, it would be because someone broke those rules. It would not be because the risk was unmanageable. It would be because someone decided not to manage it.

When you think about it, we all manage a wide variety of risks in our everyday lives. Driving a car on the freeway could be life threatening if we don't follow the rules that are designed to help us manage that risk. That's why we manage the risks of driving at high speeds by keeping our eyes open, driving defensively, wearing seat belts, and keeping our speed within reasonable boundaries.

Putting a 747 airplane in the air has a lot of obvious risks. It weighs a million pounds, carries a lot of people...yet we trust it to fly us safely at 40,000 feet traveling 500 miles per hour. Why do we trust stepping onto a plane like that? Because we know the government has strict safety requirements and the pilots have intense education and experience. All those risks and more have been considered and proactively managed.

So we can see that it's not necessary to avoid risk to keep ourselves safe. It's also not necessary to just throw caution to the wind and hope for the best. Instead, we need to understand the risks before us and learn how to manage them. That's the key to prospering with any type of investing activity.

KEY POINT!
There are 3 approaches to dealing with risk

Try to avoid risk	Take risk	Manage risk

Let's walk through the most common types of risks facing investors so you'll know what they are and how you can control them in your own investing.

Non-Systemic Risk

Non-systemic risks are the things that can happen to affect the price of an individual stock without impacting the overall market.

For example, when British Petroleum (BP) caused a big oil spill in the Gulf of Mexico, it had a fast and harsh impact on its stock price. BP stock went—very quickly—from $60 to $30 a share. But the overall market felt very little negative impact from this event. The spill didn't impact the entire system.

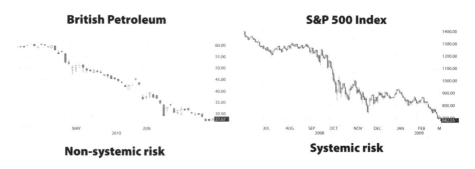

Non-systemic risk   **Systemic risk**

When a company manufactures products, those products can have defects. Should there be a recall on brake pads for your car, or a particular toy, or some other product, it will likely affect the price of that company's stock. But there's no reason for investors to think the company's problem will bring down the entire market. Not even a company as big as BP, not even with an event as big as that spill. That is a non-systemic risk.

Financial advisors will often tell their clients to protect themselves against non-systemic risk by diversifying. This type of diversification will help an investor absorb the impact of an individual stock that may go down if some kind of non-systemic event should occur. This isn't necessarily a bad approach. But it does concern me when investors use this approach of diversification and are satisfied because they think they have managed *all* their risks.

The truth is, they have only addressed one type of risk. And by diversifying across other stocks in various sectors, they are actually exposing themselves to risk from another source: systemic risk.

Systemic Risk

As we just discussed, most investors think that diversifying across multiple stocks protects their risk exposure. If one stock goes down, the others can help prop up the losses.

BUILD ON IT

PILLAR #4: Risk Diversification does not protect against systemic risk.

There's just one problem with only focusing on *non-systemic risk*. What happens when the entire market drops? How does diversification help your retirement account when nearly every single stock takes a plunge.

This isn't just a theoretical possibility. This is the reality we have been living with over the past few years. Take a look at the following chart to see the difference between non-systemic and systemic risk:

On the left is the example of British Petroleum we talked about earlier. We can see that after the oil spill in the Gulf of Mexico, the stock price rapidly lost half of its value.

On the right is a different chart that shows the broader market (represented by the S&P 500) dropping due to the sub-prime meltdown. This market drop was the result of factors that hurt the overall market. Here's the short version: The Federal Reserve lowered interest rates so people could borrow money more easily. As a result, people did indeed borrow money at rapid rates and invested that money in houses and others things. This buying frenzy quickly drove up the prices of real estate to levels that weren't realistic. It didn't take long for this demand to drop as investors realized things had gotten out of hand. Suddenly, people weren't able to make their mortgage payments and they weren't able to sell the properties for anywhere near what they paid. That's when the real estate bubble popped, and the resulting mortgage meltdown brought the entire stock market and most of the economy down with it.

In the chart on the right, we can see that the S&P went from over 1,400 down to 700. In less than two years, half the value of the market disappeared into thin air. Many investors lost 50 percent of their account values. The same thing happened in 2000 when the dot-com bubble burst. It brought the whole system down with it.

That's why it's called **systemic risk.** Something happens beyond an investor's control and it affects the entire market system. If you were invested in the market during this time, it doesn't matter how diversified you were; it's likely that most of your stocks lost much of their value.

As a reminder, this is why we focused earlier in the book on carefully doing our fundamental analysis. Analyzing fundamentals is one of our best tools for recognizing the degree of systemic risk we can expect. When we see the government printing money or the condition of a government's financial statement, we can use that information to help us measure the amount of risk we would face when investing in stocks tied to that system. Remember, even quality stocks can be vulnerable to systemic risks.

KEY POINT!

Sovereign debt crisis increases systemic risk

In Japan, the Nikkei lost 14 percent from 1984 to 2012. Even with big-name companies such as Toyota, Sony, and others, the Japanese system has been losing money for nearly 30 years. That isn't good news for Japanese investors who have had their retirement accounts in the market and are hoping for good returns.

European countries are struggling with debt loads and austerity measures in an attempt to get their economies back under control. In the United States, the debt/GDP ratio is getting out of control. The risk of investing in those systems is going up. And because we're looking at systemic risk, we as investors need to be aware of it so we can control our exposure. We don't want to lose money.

Purchase Risk

Purchase risk is a simple concept tied to the currency of your specific country. If the value of your currency is dropping, what risks do you face by hanging onto your money?

What if you put one dollar into the bank today, and a year from now the value is still at one dollar? At face value you might be disappointed that you didn't earn anything in interest, but you might not care too much because you still have your dollar. But consider this in the face of rising prices of goods you might have purchased during the same time period.

For example, if a gallon of gasoline was one dollar at the beginning of the same period, but increased to ten dollars per gallon a year later, what does that mean for your money? You have actually lost a lot of *buying power* during that time. This is what we call *purchase risk*.

When considering the state of the economy, do we see the value of our currency falling? Is our money best held in cash or in another investment that will better hold its value?

Other Risks to Consider

We've addressed some of the major risks that stock market investors typically face, but those are by no means the only types of risks that are out there. It's vital to do your homework for a particular investment to know what risks might stand in your way. Some of these risks are *obsolescence risk, geographic risk, interest rate risk, political risk, longevity risk, legislative risk*...the names alone give you an idea of what dangerous waters might await you. But with the right education, you can navigate those waters successfully.

Controlling Your Risk

Remember when we discussed how most investors put their money into investments and cross their fingers that everything goes their way? That's not investing, it's hoping. And when you put your money behind that hope you're not investing, you're gambling.

KEY POINT!
"Hope" = no control
"I hope unemployment improves"
"I hope my stock price makes a comeback"
"I hope I can retire"
"I hope the market recovers"

Life is already full of so many things we can't control. First of all, we can't control the market or the direction of a stock. We can't control natural disasters—a tsunami in Japan, an earthquake in Mexico, Hurricane Katrina in New Orleans. We can't control the outcome of events we know about in advance—earnings reports or FDA approvals. As individuals we certainly can't control sovereign issues, like debt and fiscal policy.

If you are in a mutual fund, all of these things affect you yet there's nothing you can do about them. You're taking a lot of risks, betting on a long-term diversified portfolio, and hoping that everything will work out and it will all be rosy. And often, even though your account statement shows you that it's not really working out the way you envisioned, you still keep hoping.

On the other hand, there are many things in our lives that we can have control over.

- You can't control the weather, but you *can* control where you build your house to hopefully avoid hurricanes, floods, and tornadoes.

- You can't control the market going up and down, but you *can* control how you position yourself in that market.

- You can't control if your house burns down, but you *can* take precautions to minimize the chance of it catching fire and control whether or not you purchase insurance.

Insurance

When we possess things that are important to us, such as our homes, cars, and investments, one of the best ways to protect them is with insurance. And even with precautionary measures, sometimes accidents happen. If we just hope that our house doesn't burn down, it may still happen and we'll be out of luck. Yet if we buy insurance on that house, at least our investment is protected. It may be inconvenient, but it's nice to know that we can be back in a newly rebuilt home within a matter of months. When we buy insurance on our investments, we know what the outcome will be. We have control over the situation. That gives an investor a lot more peace of mind than does hope.

KEY POINT!	
Risk is related to control	
No control	**Total control**
Information (FA & TA)	**Positioning**
Stock market direction	**Buying insurance**
Major economic events	**Position size**
Corporate policies	**Asset allocation**
Fiscal and monetary policies	**Exit strategy**
	Personal financial policy
	Financial education

That's how professional investors maintain their ability to grow wealth no matter what happens. They plan for the best, and also plan for the worst. Since they can't control the market direction, they insure their investment with a hedge.

BUILD ON IT

**PILLAR #4: Risk
A hedge is insurance on an investment.**

Whenever you have something you can't control, you can usually **insure** it. You can't control Hurricane Katrina, but you can have insurance on your house. You can't control a tsunami, but you can have insurance on your business. You can't control a market crash, but you can have insurance, or a *hedge,* on your portfolio. That's the big secret. If I can't control it, I need to hedge it or insure it. I can't do anything about the sovereign stuff, but I can control my **personal fiscal policy**. If you want to gamble, go to Vegas—and never bet more than you are prepared to lose. Because gambling is entertainment; it's *not* an investment.

Exit

Another way to manage risk in an investment is to plan an exit strategy. This is a pre-determined plan to get out of a stock when it hits certain levels. This can be tough to do in other asset classes such as real estate, because they're not as liquid as the stock market. There are even some paper assets that lack liquidity and where having an exit strategy might be difficult. However, for most large companies with highly traded stocks, an exit strategy is a viable risk management tool.

BUILD ON IT

PILLAR #4: Risk
Having an exit strategy
(a plan to get out of a stock when
it hits a certain level) is a powerful
risk management tool.

Before entering a trade, you can set the price points at which you want to automatically exit the trade. If it does poorly, you don't want to sit on that stock for a long time—you want to get out as quickly as possible to minimize your losses. That's one of the great advantages of owning stock: If you don't like the trade, you can just click a button and exit it instantly. In fact, most exit strategies these days can be programmed into your computer and you can give precise instructions to the brokerage. These instructions can be very specific and detailed with many "if/then" statements that allow you to go about your life rather than babysitting your investments all day long.

It's no surprise that the best investors are those with the best financial education. When you know how to plan for virtually any investing scenario, you can structure your plan in your favor. Every investor makes the decision on whether they will invest in ignorance or if they'll become educated. It's a choice. Trust me, doing nothing...being ignorant? That's a choice too. And it's the most dangerous one of all.

Whether you are interested in either cash flow or capital gains investing, having a good understanding of the different risk-management strategies available to you is a very smart move. You'd be surprised how far ahead of the novice investor you are just in knowing about hedging and exit strategies. But there is a lot more to get excited about when it comes to risk management.

Risk/Reward Ratio

In our study of technical analysis, we learned a little about how to look at the price movement of a stock on a chart to set a price target, an entry point, and an exit. To help us evaluate the potential attractiveness of one trade over another we can use these price targets and entry/exit points as a way to measure each trade. We call this measurement the *risk/reward ratio.*

5 Basic Points to Identify

Target
Set a target that is *likely* to be achieved

Entry
Enter when the stock fits your *criteria*

Exit
Plan your exit point, *before* you enter the position

Target — 120
— 130
— 110

Entry — 100
Exit — 90
— 80

Reward — The reward is the distance between the entry and target

Risk — The risk is the distance between the entry and the exit

- **Reward** = The amount of money you expect to profit when entering the trade. This is usually shown as the price target you expect the stock to reach while you are in the trade.

- **Risk** = The amount of money you are willing to risk losing in order to be in the trade. This is usually shown as the price at which you pre-set your exit point when entering a trade.

KEY POINT!

It's vital to know the maximum risk of any investment.

When we speak of risk / reward ratios we refer to the amount of money lost when the stock is sold at the exit price.

The maximum risk is the total value of the shares.

We can show this mathematically as:

Risk/Reward Ratio = Anticipated Profits : Anticipated Losses

For example, let's say we are considering buying a stock that is currently at $10 per share. After doing our technical analysis, we think that a target price of $12 is realistic. On the risk side, we understand that the stock might drop slightly on its way up to the target level so we're comfortable putting our stop-loss exit at $9 to give a dollar's worth of wiggle room. In this scenario, our risk/reward ratio looks like this:

$$(\$12 - \$10) : (\$10 - \$9) = 2 : 1 \text{ ratio}$$

In other words, we think this trade has the potential to earn twice as much in profits as we stand to lose.

But what does this mean if we compare it to another potential stock buy?

As you analyze other potential stocks in the same way, you can quickly find and compare the different risk/reward ratios. A stock investor who is seeking a capital gain might establish criteria of having a minimum of $2 in reward for every $1 risk that they take. The idea here is that if the investor makes ten trades and half are winners, that investor can still come out ahead because of the risk/reward ratio.

For options traders this ratio can be significantly less because of the amount of leverage available in those instruments.

For cash flow investors this ratio is based on the amount of cash flow they received for the amount of money placed at risk.

There's no magic number where one size fits all when it comes to a risk/reward ratio. Investors will develop their own criteria based on tolerance for risk and other factors such as age and investment goals. It is an individual process.

Exit Strategies

You may be asking the question, "Why have an exit strategy? Why not just buy a stock and hold it until it grows?" That's what most of us have been taught—that smart investing is to buy and hold for the long term. Like I said before, it's a matter of control and risk management. Since you cannot control how a company manages itself or what will happen to its stock price, you need to be very careful in how you invest with that company.

For example, take a look at the following list of major companies that have gone bankrupt in the recent past. This is just a small list, yet we can see that the combined value of these losses is more than $1.6 trillion. That isn't funny money. That huge amount represents losses experienced by real investors like you and me. And it's the best reason I can think of to have an exit strategy every time you make an investment.

Notable Bankruptcies

Lehman Brothers	**$691 billion**
Washington Mutual	**$327.9 billion**
WorldCom	**$103.9 billion**
General Motors	**$91 billion**
CIT	**$71 billion**
Enron	**$65.5 billion**
Conseco	**$61 billion**
Chrysler LLC	**$39 billion**
Pacific Gas and Electric Co.	**$36.1 billion**
Texaco	**$34.9 billion**
Global Crossing, Ltd.	**$30.1 billion**
Lucent Technologies	**$26 billion.**
United Air lines	**$25.1 billion**

Even though some of these companies were able to restructure and are back in business, the shareholders still lost their money.

Another reason to have a good exit strategy is to avoid big losses to your trading account that can take a long time from which to recover. Whether they realize it or not, buy-and-hold investors have made the decision to hold onto their stocks through bad times and good. They hope that in the long run, everything will go in their favor.

Let me show you a simple illustration of how this line of thinking can be very detrimental to your long-term success plans. Suppose you hold a particular stock that is worth $100 per share today. If something unforeseen happens, such as when British Petroleum had the Gulf oil spill, that stock could lose half of its value almost overnight. Suddenly, you have lost half your wealth in that stock. In order for that stock to return to its previous value, it needs to double itself—it requires a 100 percent growth rate just to get back to even. For a stock that grows at perhaps 6-7 percent annually, that can take a long time.

This is not a far-fetched scenario. Let's take a look at how Microsoft dropped after the dot-com bubble burst in 1999. At the beginning of that time period, Microsoft was trading around $51–$52. In 2011 it had dropped to around $25. That's a 50 percent loss for an investor holding that stock. Now it has to achieve a 100 percent run to get back up there.

Why Exit Strategy Instead Of Buy And Hold?

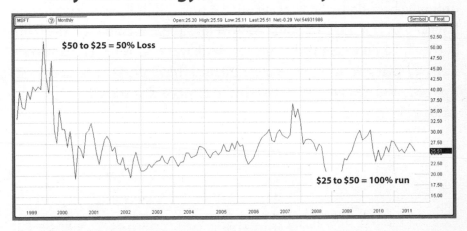

As we have seen, it's much easier for stocks to drop quickly than to rise. That's why it can be wise for us to have a smart exit strategy in place to get out of stocks before we lose much. Then we'll be better positioned to take advantage of prices when they're on the way back up. Smart investors take advantage of this knowledge to keep their profits rising.

Entering Trade Orders for Protection

Now that you can see that buying and holding isn't a surefire way for you to grow wealth, how can you protect yourself from dangerous price drops? And how can you lock in your profits to maximize success? It's actually very fast and easy to build in these safety factors when you place your trades. Thanks to today's computerization of the entire trading process, it's simply a matter of knowing the terms and entering the values into your software.

To show you how this is done, let's look at a sample trade, ACME. As we look at the chart on the right, we decide that a target price of $45 is realistic. Currently, ACME is moving down a bit, but we don't expect that to continue very far. We've drawn a support line on the chart that's slightly lower than the current price of $38.83. So we're comfortable waiting a day or two to make sure the price bounces off that support and comes back up. If it continues down past the support level, we don't want to be in the trade. The ideal is to enter the trade at $39 as it rises.

If the price does as expected and we enter our long position on the way up at $39, we need to recognize that it could also reverse and begin dropping back down. So we want an exit point slightly below the support level at $37. If it hits that point, we will lose a couple dollars on the trade, but we'll be protected if the stock slides lower over time. For this trade scenario, that gives us a reward of $6.00 for a risk of $2. The lowest reward/risk ratio you should ever consider is 2:1. Since this trade gives us a 3:1 ratio, we're in good shape.

Orders to Open

For our trade transaction, we want to put in an order for an entry point at $39 and an exit point at $37.

On the left is a broker's order page. Each broker's page looks slightly different, but they all have the same components. Online order forms help you give instructions to the brokerage regarding what you want to do. You can put in orders to open a position or orders to close a position. In this case, you are going to buy 100 shares of ACME. This is an entry order to open a long position.

Brokerages allow you to specify exactly how you want to enter your positions. As you will see, you can have as much control as you want when entering orders. When placing an order, you usually have at least four different order types to choose from:

Market Order: This means the trade will go through right now at the current price or at whatever price the market opens at if you place the order outside of trading hours. But since we have a specific entry point we want, we won't use the market order option. In fact, I rarely use market orders when I trade because it requires that I give up an amount of control, which, of course, is not always a good idea.

Limit Order: Many people make a mistake here. If I fill in $39 here, I'm saying I want to buy this at $39 or higher. But I don't want to buy it at $40 or $41 because that screws up my reward/risk ratio. I want it at exactly $39.

I could say I want it at $39 or lower, but that might put me in too early. It's at $38.83 today so this order would trigger the trade now, while the stock is going down. I don't want to automatically buy a stock that is going down. This is one of the most common mistakes people make when they enter orders. They think they're really smart because there is a chance they will get it cheaper. But they are buying stocks that are headed the wrong way.

I want stocks that are headed up.

Stop Market Order: The next order we can select is the *stop market* order. Now this is an interesting order. This brings in a window for a *stop* price. It means, "Stop and don't do anything until it reaches $39." I think this is confusing because it really means "Go" since the order will be triggered when the stock reaches $39. But again, soon after it hits $39, it might go to $39.05 or it might go to $38.06. The order will be triggered as soon as $39 is reached, even if the price then drops down or gaps up. I don't use this type of order much either.

Stop Limit Order: To get very precise control over entering a trade I most often use the *stop limit*. This requires you to enter two prices, the stop price and the limit price. I am now giving an order to buy when the stock reaches $39, but I am also limiting the price to $39 or higher, so that if it suddenly gaps up to $41 and reduces my reward, the order will not trigger. Once the order has been triggered and I'm in, I need to put in an exit order to limit my loss and manage my risk. Controlling this risk, limiting losses, is what this is all about.

With practice, all this can become second nature.

For an exit order you can put in a stop market order, an order to sell if the stock hits $37. So, the *stop limit* is the very specific point where I want to enter the trade, and the *stop market* is where I want to bail out for safety.

Order To Exit

Protective Put Options

Is it possible that a stock price could 'jump' over your exit price? Absolutely. This can happen around earnings announcements or other newsworthy events such as a pharmaceutical company failing to gain FDA approval for new a drug. This is another place where an education in options will be valuable.

At this point, you know how options can be used to generate cash flow. For serious investors, options also can be used as insurance on their investment positions. For example, if you are investing in a company that has an erratic stock price that jumps around a lot, a good insurance policy can protect you in the event those jumps don't go your way.

A good example of this kind of stock was Research in Motion (RIMM), makers of the Blackberry phone and other electronic devices and services. This particular stock had a tendency to gap, meaning its stock price made huge jumps or drops in price that appear to leave gaps on a chart. Much of the time investors can see these coming on the earnings calendar. If you happened to have a long position in a stock like this and have your safety stops in place for protection, what would happen if the stock gapped right over your stop? Suppose you entered a stop at $34.50, but the gap meant that your stop triggered much lower at $29.50 (the next price after it gapped). Suddenly, you are facing a loss you didn't expect.

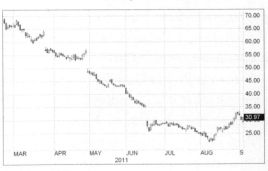

Exp	Symbol	Last	Bid	Ask	Net
Oct11 22.00	O:RIMM 11V22.00	0.59	0.58	0.60	-0.07
Oct11 23.00	O:RIMM 11V23.00	0.74	0.73	0.75	-0.11
Oct11 24.00	O:RIMM 11V24.00	0.91	0.91	0.93	-0.20
Oct11 25.00	O:RIMM 11V25.00	1.12	1.12	1.14	-0.19
Oct11 26.00	O:RIMM 11V26.00	1.37	1.37	1.39	-0.27
Oct11 27.00	O:RIMM 11V27.00	1.72	1.66	1.69	-0.16
Oct11 28.00	O:RIMM 11V28.00	2.01	2.00	2.03	-0.22
Oct11 29.00	O:RIMM 11V29.00	2.39	2.39	2.42	-0.25
Oct11 30.00	O:RIMM 11V30.00	2.83	2.85	2.86	-0.27
Oct11 31.00	O:RIMM 11V31.00	3.34	3.30	3.40	-0.36
Oct11 32.00	O:RIMM 11V32.00	3.85	3.85	3.90	-0.35
Oct11 32.50	O:RIMM 11V32.50	5.45	4.10	4.25	-2.10
Oct11 33.00	O:RIMM 11V33.00	4.40	4.45	4.55	-0.40
Oct11 34.00	O:RIMM 11V34.00	5.40	5.10	5.20	-0.07
Oct11 35.00	O:RIMM 11V35.00	5.95	5.80	5.85	-0.40
Oct11 37.00	O:RIMM 11V37.00	7.45	7.30	7.40	0.20

$3.40
For the choice
to SELL RIMM
@ $31
Before Exp
(OCT 2011)

RIMM Sept 6, 2011

To protect ourselves against a situation like this, we can buy a *protective put option* on the stock in order to insure it until after the earnings announcement. We can enter into an agreement with another person where that person agrees to buy the stock at a certain strike price within a certain period of time, and we have the option to sell it.

BUILD ON IT

PILLAR #4: Risk
Protective put options are when others agree to buy stock at a certain strike price within a certain period of time, and are an effective way to protect against drops in the price of your stock.

On the left here we have the October option chain for RIMM. Suppose it's now September 4th, so we have about five weeks before the October expiration date. As we look at the puts we see the ask is $3.40 for the option, meaning that for a premium of $3.40 we can insure $30 worth of stock for the next five weeks. At 10 percent of the stock price, this insurance policy may seem expensive. But the reason for the higher-than-usual option price is the frequent gaps in RIMM's stock price.

After we purchase the option to sell the stock at $31, what happens if it gaps down to $26? The protective put option guarantees that we can sell it for $31. Even if the stock were to somehow fall to zero during the life of the option, we could still sell it for $31.

Sure enough, RIMM went down once again. By the option expiration date in October it was trading in the low $20s. The put option certainly would have helped soften the blow.

Protective put options can be an effective way to protect against stocks and markets with extreme volatility. Many of the high-flying stocks like RIMM have fallen to trade in the single digits after being worth well over $100 a share. These dramatic falls have cost many investors much of their fortune, while other savvy investors used insurance and hedges to mitigate the risk of such meltdowns.

RIMM Sept 6, 2011

**$3.40
For the choice
to SELL RIMM
@ $31
Before Exp
(OCT 2011)**

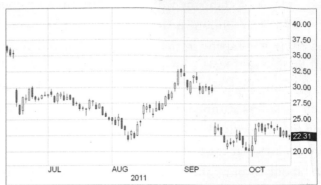

How Hedging Saved Mark Cuban's Fortune

Mark Cuban became an Internet billionaire after selling his company to Yahoo! for $5.7 billion in stock. Sounds like a fairy tale ending, right? Not long after, though, the dot-com bubble burst and the market crashed. In just five months, Yahoo!'s shares dropped 90 percent.

Yahoo During The Dot Com Bust

You can see from the chart how most of the value was wiped out. Did Mark Cuban lose all that money? No, because he had hedged the stock against such a loss. This simple act of protecting himself made him look like a genius.

253

Steve Kroft did an interview with Cuban on *60 Minutes* where Kroft said, "He had a company worth $15 million in revenue and one year later it sold for $5.7 billion in stock." That's a pretty cool day. You take your $15 million company in the dot-com boom and you're cranking out $5.7 billion in stock. Notice he didn't sell it for cash; he sold it for stock.

Cuban laughed and said, "Boy, it's as shocking to me now as it was then." He was stunned it happened to him, but not so stunned that he stopped thinking. Kroft says, "More than 300 employees also became millionaires—at least on paper. But Cuban, sensing the Internet bubble was about to burst, made his shrewdest move. He began unloading his Yahoo! stock, using a hedging strategy that would lock in his profits. 'I was covered,' says Cuban, 'and then some.'"

Unloading means he sold his stock, and, as you know, *hedging* means he insured against loss. Most likely, Cuban bought put options or some other hedge. *Put options* would have given him the option to sell the stock high even though the stock went right down to almost nothing. While Yahoo! was heading down, Mark Cuban would have been able to sell at the high prices of the past.

And notice the language, "I was covered," he says, "and then some." So he was insured and, apparently, according to him, for more than the stock was worth. Can you insure your home for more than it's worth? Definitely, if you want to pay the premium. From his words, it appears that Cuban was over-insured and he actually made money on Yahoo!'s downward spiral.

Remember, *hedging* is just buying insurance on your investment. When you have insurance, you can look like a genius no matter what happens. If Yahoo!'s price had gone up, Cuban would have been a genius for selling his company for stock. But when Yahoo! went down, he looked like a genius for planning ahead and having a hedge.

This is a great example of how good risk management made someone look smart, but I think it's the opposite. Mark Cuban would have been a fool not to hedge that stock. Think of how many people were financially punished during market crashes without any kind of insurance on their investments. Markets can burn to the ground just like houses. If you're shrewd, you have insurance. That doesn't take genius; it's just common sense.

For the investor looking to generate cash flow and protect assets, buying options is an excellent tool. It gives us very specific control in environments that buy-and-hold investing isn't able to offer. Plus, it can serve as insurance for virtually any stock-investing scenario.

Correlating Assets

Some people think they are safe because they have many different stocks and mutual funds. As you look at your charts, with your advisors, you might find something that you never expected: Many mutual fund charts are nearly identical copies of each other. This can be a great lesson about diversification. Some folks think they are safe through buying a number of different funds. In other words, if these funds are all correlated to the overall market they often have the same movement.

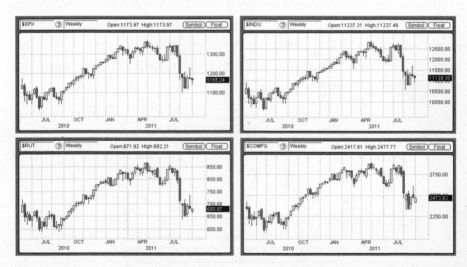

Look at the charts above to see correlation in action. Some people believe they are spreading their risk around, but often they find that their mutual fund is not much different than if they had been investing in these individual indexes. As you can see, though, the indexes essentially follow each other because they are the mirrors of overall market behavior.

The trades might seem different because they are at different price levels, and because there will be different strikes and different premiums. But they're all correlated together and follow the same movement. They go up together, and they go down together. The investor who unwittingly invests in *correlating assets* is very exposed.

Correlating assets don't offer us an opportunity to hedge against each other. This is why our discussion of systemic risk versus non-systemic risk is so important. If you are diversified across correlating assets, then you are very much exposed to systemic risk!

Inverse Correlating Assets

Now let's look at two new charts: the S&P 100 and the VXX. The VXX is a short-term measure of the VIX, the volatility index. Notice this inverse correlation on the charts. You can see that these charts move directly opposite of each other. When the S&P is up, the VXX is down. And when the S&P falls, the VXX rises. This is an obvious example of two *inverse-correlating assets*. Before investing in either, we would need to do more research. But seeing them in this sharp contrast helps us understand this non-correlating concept.

I would never buy the VXX as a long position any more than I would hope to make money on my car insurance. Some investors simply use it, sometimes, as investment insurance. Long ago I had positions in the S&P when the market began falling apart. My analysis had told me that the market was likely to go sideways, but I decided to protect myself in case things became more unstable. I knew that the VXX was negatively correlated with the S&P, so I decided to use the VXX as a hedge.

Here's what happened: When the S&P dropped, I lost some money. But my hedge in the VXX soared and earned thousands of dollars for me. The S&P fell 20 percent, but the VXX doubled. In that situation, I was able to insure against risk and also earned a good profit by using a non-correlated asset against my main investment.

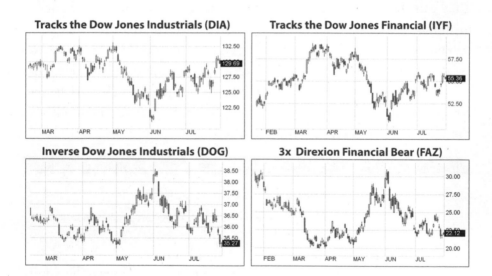

Now look at these two pairs. They are exact mirrors of each other. On the upper left is the Dow Jones Industrial Average (DIA), called *diamonds* for short. Below that is the DOG, which is the inverse of the DJIA, called the *dog*.

On the right is the Dow Jones Financial Sector Index Fund (IYF) and the inverse correlation below it is the Direxion Daily Financial Bear 3X Shares (FAZ).

Better yet, you can buy an inexpensive call on the FAZ for even greater leverage. If the IYF tanks, you know the FAZ will go through the roof and you have massive leverage with your call option.

In my own investing, I continually use non-correlating assets to manage my risk. Entering trades into non-correlating assets gives you one level of risk management. One asset goes down, but the other asset goes up. You can then add a second level of risk management with *protective options* on your trades.

Buying Investments in Pairs

When people purchase a home it's almost never an isolated purchase. They pair the home with an insurance policy. To buy a home without fire insurance is foolish. Even though the chance of fire might be small, it is still out of the owner's control, and the chances of total devastation are too great. So it makes sense to have a hedge to protect anything of value. That is something almost everyone can relate to. Yet in the stock market, very few people use hedges. Most folks buy the primary investment without the secondary purchase for protection.

KEY POINT!

Consider investing in pairs.

When investors take a position in a primary investment, they often take a small but leveraged position in a secondary investment to hedge the primary investment.

While most people see it as common practice to protect the equity in their home with insurance, almost nobody thinks about hedging their 401(k) or IRA. Yet which is more likely to burn down in the next five years?

Position Sizing

Casinos are smart. They make a lot of money. But they do this by controlling risk. And there's much we can learn from how they go about controlling risk. Here are two keys to consider.

- They strictly limit the amount they can lose in a single bet (table limits)
- They win more often than they lose (mathematical odds)

One thing they need to watch out for is big bets. Imagine you're in a game of blackjack and a new player comes to the table with some serious cash. He drops millions of dollars down on the table, gets one lucky hand, and walks away...wiping the casino out.

The casino just can't allow that. They have to put limits on what they can lose, so they have to limit what their guests can do. Casinos make gamblers spread their money out over smaller bets and over a period of time (and they have a ton of clever ways to get gamblers to do just that) with table limits. That way, the casino allows the mathematical odds to work in their favor. That is why every casino game has a *table limit* that limits the size of each bet. The casinos know they are going to make money, because they limit how much they can lose in each hand and the math takes care of the rest.

Table limits also help them manage the risk they face with gamblers who try a strategy of doubling down. Let's say the gambler places a bet and loses $5. He places a bet of $10 next time and if he wins he gets his $5 back plus more. If he loses, then he is down $15. A win on a $30 bet, and he gets back his $15 plus more. So these guys just keep doubling down, $100, $500, $1,000, $2,000. As long as they keep betting bigger and bigger, sooner or later they'll win and get back everything they've lost, and more—unless there is a table limit.

You and I can use the same strategy to limit how much of our total account is at risk in any one trade. This is called *position sizing*. If you decide that you do not want to risk any more than 1% of you account in any one trade, then look at the risk/reward ratio we studied earlier and adjust the number of shares you trade accordingly.

The Power of Probabilities

In reality, the casino's games of chance have more to do with math than chance. In reality, casinos leave nothing to chance. A good example is what they do with roulette, a game of win-loss percentage. With 18 red spaces, 18 black spaces, and two green spaces, the casino has the advantage.

- A bet on black, and the player has 18 chances to win and 20 chances to lose

- A bet on red, and the player has 18 chances to win and 20 chances to lose

- A bet on green, and the player has two chances to win and 36 chances to lose

Even with this clear advantage, the casino will lose some bets here and there. But they will always win far more than they lose. Now combine that with a table limit. They closely analyze and control these numbers to give them an advantage—and for the casino that means earnings.

So why don't you do the same with each trade? Why don't you set a limit? Why don't you create your own positive win-loss percentage?

The answer is you can do all of those things. How do you get a win-loss percentage to increase? By becoming proficient in fundamental analysis, technical analysis, and continued education. Learn the charts. Trade with the trends. Learn to see what's most likely. Place trades that have a high probability of paying off.

How do you limit losses? The stock market equivalent of a table limit is called position size.

Suppose you have an account of $100,000 and you determine that your risk tolerance is 1 percent. It could be 2 percent or 0.5 percent, but for now we'll stick with 1 percent. So the risk in a trade as far as your stop loss is concerned is $1,000, which is 1 percent of your total account.

You want to enter a long position at $39 and put in a stop-loss exit at $37. That means you could lose $2 in this trade. Under your position-size rule, the most you are prepared to risk is $1,000. So the largest position size you can take is 500 shares. This doesn't mean you have to buy 500 shares, but it does mean you aren't buying more than 500 shares. With this limit, if you must exit the position at your exit point of $37 you won't lose more than $1,000. So if it goes against you and you lose it, you still have $99,000. Just as a table limit keeps the casino in business, your position size allows you to trade another day.

If, on the other hand, you hit your target of $45, you'll have made $3,000. This is more than survival; this is prosperity.

So, you do the fundamentals, you do the technicals, and you spread the trades around non-correlated assets. For the sake of argument, let's say that with your 10 trades, maybe you'll get a 50:50 win/loss ratio. Do the math. Five trades that earn you $3,000 each, and five trades that lose you $1,000 each.

That's an over-simplification, but it sums up the basic idea. With education and experience you will improve your percentage of winners to losers. You will limit your position size so that you are only risking a minimal percentage of your account in any one trade.

The more trades you do—and the higher the percentage of winners to losers and the greater your reward to risk ratio—the less you stand to lose.

The Risk Management Toolbox

<u>Basic risk management toolbox</u>

Solid Fundamental and Technical Analysis skills

Proper risk/reward ratios

Stop-loss orders and exits

Protective put and call options

Inversely leveraged assets

Non-correlating assets

Position sizing

Take a moment and think about how you have managed risk in the past as compared to what you have read in this chapter. Review this basic risk management toolbox. You have seen how, by setting a target, you can calculate the reward you are aiming for and decide how much risk you are prepared to take to get that reward.

We have introduced the idea of placing *stop loss orders* so that your exit order will be triggered if the trade turns against you, thus limiting your losses.

We have looked at how you can use *protective options* to insure against loss, just as you insure your house against fire. You hope it doesn't happen but, if it does, you're covered.

You have seen how to pick *non-correlating assets* to manage the risk. If one of your trades tanks, all the others won't necessarily tank with it.

We have looked at *position sizing*, deciding on the size of your trade based on the potential loss and what percentage of your account you are prepared to risk in a single trade.

And what has this all been about? It has been about controlling the risk, managing the risk. It's been about the difference I started section, this pillar, with: a comparison between the person who swaggers and says, "Oh yeah, I bought this stock and it went sky high." and the man or woman who says, "I was in this investment and the thing tanked, and this is how I minimized my losses."

You can appreciate that success is not about getting lucky. It's about minimizing losses and controlling risk.

And that brings us to education itself as a means to control risk. For students like you and me, education is the most important investment we can make.

Education

One of my pet peeves with the investment industry is that too often they remove the investor from the investing equation. This reminds me of an experience I had growing up when I was cut from the high school basketball team the very first year I tried out. I was tall, but I was also pretty skinny and less coordinated than other players. I had a goal to play in college. But most people suggested that I find a different goal because less than 1 percent of athletes play sports at the college level. By suggesting my odds were less that 1 in 100, they removed me from the equation. They didn't think of asking me if I was willing to out-work or out-practice 100 people. It was as if they assumed that I could have no impact—no control—on whether or not I accomplished the goal. Chance becomes less of a factor when hard work and training are placed into the equation.

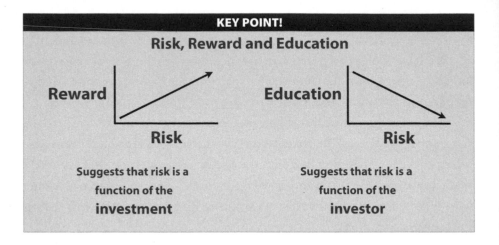

This odds-maker approach is similar to the traditional view of risk and reward. People start at the bottom with the things they feel are 'safe,' cash, treasuries—low risk, low reward investments. Stocks…"Oh, but stocks can be risky." Options, "No, I don't go for big rewards, it's too risky." People think anyone trading the FOREX Market is nuts. The investment industry has dismissed the fact that investors can have an impact on their success…simply by *educating* themselves.

The traditional view is that to get the big leveraged rewards at the top, you have to push way up on the risk scale.

Ask yourself: Is a BMW a safe car? What if the driver is intoxicated?

Like I've said, it's not the vehicle alone that determines the risk. It's who the driver is. Certainly, trading the FOREX has significant risk. But how many good people are buying mutual funds and don't even know what systemic risk is? In my view, the people who understand all the risk in FOREX and are educated in how to manage it have a far greater chance of prosperity in their lives than the uneducated masses riding the mutual-fund roller coaster. Many of the option traders are getting more reward but they've also reduced risk because they know how to hedge it. They know how to do it. They're educated in managing risk.

Ignorance plays a big part in risk. With education you can manage the high-reward vehicles because you can also manage and control the risk. Once you have mastered a basic risk management toolbox, you will be ready to learn even more sophisticated risk management techniques such as *delta hedging* and more. The more tools you have, the more strategies you can implement, and the more opportunities you will have.

Chapter Summary

Let's review some of the important points of Chapter Seven:

1. There are three approaches to dealing with risk.

    a. Investors might try to **avoid risk**. The reality is that there is no place to put one's wealth where it is not exposed to some type of risk. Money placed in individual stocks faces non-systemic risk. Even wealth placed in diversified portfolios is often subject to systemic risk. There's risk in buying a home, but if you don't you may have no place to live.

    b. Investors might just **take risk**. Risk takers can also be gamblers. These investors might buy a home but fail to buy fire insurance.

    c. Experienced investors **manage risk**. If you buy a home you also want to buy fire insurance. Managing risk is the best approach.

2. Sovereign debt crises increase systemic risk.

    If the sovereign debt crisis in Europe and also the fiscal and monetary crisis in the United States continue it is likely that the fallout from these problems will affect more than just one or two individual companies but rather the entire market and the entire economy of the world.

3. The use of the word "hope" connotes a situation beyond our control.

    Statements like "I hope the market improves" imply that investors have been placed in a position in which that investor has no control. Wise investors position themselves where they can act—and not just be acted upon.

4. Risk is related to control.

   Lots of control means less risk. Less control means more risk. No control is equivalent to gambling.

5. It is vital to know the maximum risk of any investment.

6. Consider investing in pairs.

   When investors take a position in a primary investment, they often take a small but leveraged position in a secondary investment as a hedge.

7. Risk can be described in terms of the vehicle or in terms of the investor.

   Many traditional financial advisors will do a risk profile based on the client's tolerance for risk and then translate that into investments in cash, mutual funds, and bonds. This is an investment-centered approach. We can also look at investment risk as a function of the education level of the investor and the likelihood that the investor can make mistakes or position themselves wisely.

Chapter Eight

Your Next Steps

As you come to the final chapter of this book, I hope you realize just how much potential you have to become a proficient investor. The systemic problems that loom over the average worker trying to invest for retirement today are like severe storm clouds that are getting darker by the hour. Investing for the future would be a very sad proposition indeed if individuals didn't have the opportunities to learn and take action, take steps to take control of their financial future.

The good news is there's so much that you can do and so much you can learn. It's my hope that the many concepts, techniques, vocabulary words, and principles in this book can act as a foundation you can build upon in moving forward as you take the next steps.

The First Step: Goals

Way back at the beginning of this book, I asked you to write down your goals.

Lifestyle goals lead to financial goals or money goals, and money goals lead to education goals. It's an exciting feeling to realize that you and I can have whatever we want if we learn certain truths, then demonstrate the discipline and tenacity to bring our behavior into harmony with what we have learned.

The first important step you can take as you come to the final chapter of this book is to review your lifestyle goals, your money goals, and your education goals.

Develop the Habit of Personal Fundamental Analysis

You now know that fundamental analysis grows out of the information on a financial statement and that it gives you a clear picture of the strength of an entity. Remember that the financial statement is a result of policy. To create major changes to a financial statement requires major changes in policy.

In my life I strive to develop routines and policies that will bring good results. Like you, I sometimes stumble and make mistakes. I'm far from perfect, so when I make mistakes I often find I must renew my effort, make adjustments, and apply myself in new ways.

One of the routines and policies that you can start right away is to conduct a weekly personal fundamental analysis and use your financial statement as a guide. As you do so, you will begin to better understand how fundamental analysis works on all levels and begin to develop better personal policies that bring you the results want.

BUILD ON IT

Conduct a weekly personal fundamental analysis using your financial statement as a guide.

I also highly recommend that you have some fun while you learn by playing the board game *CASHFLOW® 101*. It's an incredible simulation and teaches personal fundamental analysis better than any book you can read.

Keep Moving Along the Education Continuum

Now that you have become familiar with all 4 Pillars of Investing, it's a great time to revisit the Education Continuum™ to see where you have progressed along the continuum and also how far you want to go. Take a moment and consider some of the things you've learned about each pillar, one at a time, and ask yourself where you are on the continuum.

The Education Continuum™

Ignorance → Awareness → Competency → Proficiency

For example, when it comes to basic sovereign fundamental analysis, where would you place yourself on the continuum? While there are surely still some things you don't know, hopefully when it comes to fundamentals, you have become very much aware of many important lessons. At the sovereign level, you should have a better grasp of things like monetary and fiscal policies and debt/GDP ratios.

When it comes to technical analysis I hope you feel you've become much more aware of the power that comes from being able to read a stock chart and have a better understanding of trends in the supply-and-demand story as it unfolds each day.

You now know that success has much more to do with how you position yourself as opposed to what happens in the markets or economy. You should have a greater awareness of leverage by debt, contract, time decay, and more.

You have become aware that risk is related to control. You now understand the difference between non-systemic risk and systemic risk... and how option contracts can offer a hedge.

But is there more we can learn? Absolutely. Always. One of the challenges to writing a book is to determine the ideal scope. Thousands upon thousands of pages could be (and have been) filled with strategies, techniques, and risks related to paper assets. I believe, however, that the most effective way to help someone transform into an investor is to give him or her a strong foundation on which to build. Remember the lessons of context and content from the beginning of the book.

Content and context depend upon each other. But they do come in a defined order. You have to change your context before you can effectively increase your content. As you continue along the Education Continuum™, always remember to expand and improve your context as you seek to gain more content.

Practice Paper Trading in a Virtual Account

Let's take a moment to revisit the Cone of Learning. Notice that the more active the learning, the more effective it is for the student.

After 2 weeks we tend to remember		Nature of Involvement
	Doing the Real Thing	
90% of what we say and do	Simulating the Real Experience	
	Doing a Dramatic Presentation	Active
	Giving a Talk	
70% of what we say	Participating in a Discussion	
	Seeing it Done on Location	
50% of what we hear and see	Watching a Demonstration	
	Looking at an Exhibit Watching a Demonstration	Passive
	Watching a Movie	
30% of what we see	Looking at Pictures	
20% of what we hear	Hearing Words	
10% of what we read	Reading	

Source: Cone of Learning adapted from (Dale, 1969)

Reading has always been a large part of the traditional education experience. There is great value in building your own library of important wealth books. I have to confess that I agree with the Cone of Learning in that I don't remember much of what I read, but what I do remember is valuable. For me, books are most effective in helping me develop my context and introducing me to new concepts.

And while books are a very valuable tool in introducing topics, a much more effective way to move toward proficiency along the Education Continuum™ is to do the real thing with the guidance of a mentor.

Paper trading, or virtual trading, is the practice of watching real stocks or options by using real fundamental and technical analysis and then placing imaginary positions for cash flow and risk management and then seeing how things play out. Most brokerages today offer their customers a service which enables them to open "virtual accounts" to simulate the real experience of trading.

This is a great experience designed to get you familiar with how to enter orders and test your skills—without taking any risk. If someone places an order incorrectly or makes a mistake on the order form, that type of mistake in the investing world is known as *pilot error*. Paper trading helps you cut down on your pilot errors as you become more familiar with the brokerage website or software.

Begin Building Your Investing Team

Me, my wife, and my two sons make up our family. This is my most important team. Life's challenges are much easier to tackle if it's done with a team rather than as individuals. As a family, we live our lives together and we help each other become successful, rather than trying to do everything on our own.

I've learned that teams are incredibly powerful. They allow for synergy. They offer a greater degree of safety than operating as an individual. Nearly any goal you set is more likely to be achieved if it's worked on by an entire team rather than a single individual.

I'm humbled and blessed to have been part of some incredible teams throughout my life. As a kid I was part of a Boy Scout troop. In college I was fortunate to be a part a very successful basketball team. When I was diagnosed with cancer I was treated by an entire medical team. Certainly, there were certain things that only I could do, as an individual. But I'm humbly grateful to acknowledge that success in my life has comes as the result of my team much more than anything I could have done alone.

Today I'm similarly humbled to be a small part of an education team. Robert and Kim Kiyosaki, along with the other Rich Dad Advisors, are part of a team with a common mission: to transform people's lives by giving them opportunities for financial education. The Rich Dad mission is to improve the financial wellbeing of humanity through financial education.

As you develop your team, consider your mission and the type of people you want around you. Being part of a team is a two-fold experience: to help and be helped. I've heard Robert say countless times that "investing is a team sport." Most people try to go through life on their own without a team of attorneys and accountants and advisers to help along the way. I think that's a mistake. Having a team of advisers does not mean that we try to compensate for our own ignorance by pawning off finance responsibilities and decisions to other people. On the contrary, I learn from my advisers and am very much involved and aware of what's going on—and why it's happening.

As a basketball player I understood my role on the team. I could not just coast along and expect everyone else to score all the points, play the entire defense, and do all the work. The other team members were not there because I didn't know how to play basketball. They were there to help us attain our common goal.

In addition to the attorneys and accountants as your financial advisers, consider finding effective teachers to place on your team. I can genuinely say that so much of what being a Rich Dad Advisor is all about for me is the incredible learning experience I gain from the other people on the team. It also provides the opportunity to learn more about being a teacher.

I have repeated time and again that the strength of the financial statement grows out of policy. Some people have a policy of working as a team and some people have a policy of doing things alone. Some people have an education policy and some people have a policy of ignorance. Some people have a policy of using mentors and teachers. Others have an education policy of reading books alone, instead of including practice by simulating the real experience through paper trading and playing *CASHFLOW 101*. Seeking out additional teachers and mentors is another way of practicing the real thing.

BUILD ON IT

Build an investment team.

Decide Now to Overcome Obstacles

We know that we can have anything we want in life. We know that it's just a matter of completing certain tasks each day and getting the proper education. We also know that invariably there will be things that get in our way. There will be times when we are tempted to quit...due to fatigue, failure, mistakes, frustration, input from others, or whatever. What will give you the strength to continue in the face of adversity?

I love the movie *Apollo 13*. It tells the story of United States astronauts who suffered severe damage to their spacecraft while attempting to go to the moon. These three astronauts were part of a huge NASA team on the ground. Each member of the team, whether in the space capsule or on the ground in Mission Control, faced extreme adversity, huge obstacles, and problems that were seemingly unsolvable. There's a very poignant part in the movie where members of the team approach the flight director and suggest that the problems are unsolvable. He responds with five powerful words: *failure is not an option*.

If your experience moving forward is anything like mine, you will sometimes face adversity. As much as you try to keep mistakes at a minimum, remember that mistakes are part of the education process. When you encounter adversity or obstacles, it's a good idea to go back and review your goals. That's when you will rediscover what you truly want. When you become passionate about your life and your goals, you too can say "failure is not an option."

In order to be really successful, you have to have a second gear—that reserve of energy you can go to when things get tough. Mine is my family. There will definitely be days when you and I might not want to get up and get moving in the morning. But we do not have that option. For me, I look at my wife and kids, and I find second gear pretty fast.

BUILD ON IT

Never stop learning.

Your Future Is Bright

There's a lot of doom and gloom in the world. The truth is that there are some very large and difficult problems in many parts of the world. But that doesn't mean you will become a casualty of these problems. The good news is that you can always control your position. You control your own education. You can choose to act...and not just be acted upon.

When your passive income surpasses your expenses, you're out of the Rat Race. What a place for us to be! You can get there, but you have to stop the monthly income-from-a-job circle of the Rat Race.

I hope that one of the messages you take from this book is that you can make your own personal financial statement reflect the life you choose to create. You don't need to fall victim to the problems of the world. You always control your policies.

As you move along the Education Continuum, you will begin to see more success as your efforts begin to bear fruit. You will begin to feel the satisfaction that comes from realizing what you can become and how to make it happen. Most of all, I hope you've enjoyed learning more about how paper assets can fit into your overall investing plan and how the 4 Pillars of Investing can make you a better investor, regardless of what kind of assets you plan to acquire. If you've found value in the insights in this book, I would like to continue being a member of your education team.

I know I will always keep learning and I will always keep teaching. So if you'd like to stay in touch you can do so by following me on my Facebook page, or you can drop by my website at www.stockmarketcashflow.com where you can receive regular updates on the world of paper assets as the world economy continues to change.

I wish you all the best.

About the Author

Andy Tanner is a renowned paper assets expert and successful business owner and investor known for his ability to teach key techniques for stock options investing. He serves as a coach to Rich Dad's Stock Success System trainers and as the Rich Dad Advisor for Paper Assets.

As a highly sought after educator, Andy has taught tens of thousands of investors and entrepreneurs around the world. He often speaks to students at the request of Robert Kiyosaki, showing how paper assets can fit into the Rich Dad system of investing. In 2008, Andy played a key role in developing and launching *Rich Dad's Stock Success System*, a program created to teach investors advanced technical trading techniques for profiting in both bull and bear markets.

He is the author of two books: *401(k)aos* and *Stock Market Cash Flow*, a Rich Dad Advisor series book on paper asset investing.

Andy has also created an online investing course called *The 4 Pillars of Investing*. You can find out more about it at www.4pillarsofinvesting.com.

Get free updates
from Andy

Now you can get Andy's insights on the world of investing and news events.

It's time for his new approaches and fresh ideas to help you achieve your investing and retirement goals.

Register for free updates on his web site at www.andytanner.com

RICH  DAD™
ADVISORS

Go to www.andytanner.com

RICH DAD ADVISORS

The Rich Dad Advisors series of books was created to deliver the how-to content to support Robert Kiyosaki's series of international bestsellers: *Rich Dad Poor Dad* and the Rich Dad series of books. In *Rich Dad Poor Dad*—the #1 Personal Finance Book of all Time—Robert presented the foundation for the Rich Dad principles and philosophies and set the stage for his context-changing messages that have changed the way the world thinks about money, business and investing.

The Rich Dad Advisors series of books has sold more than 2 million copies worldwide and RDA Press, exclusive publisher of the Rich Dad Advisor series and the licensor of International Rights for the series, will be releasing several new titles that will expand both the scope and depth of the series.

Rich Dad Poor Dad represents the most successful book on personal finance in our generation. Over the last 15 years, its messages have inspired millions of people and impacted tens of millions of lives in over 100 countries around the world. The Rich Dad books have continued to international bestseller lists because their messages continue to resonate with readers of all ages. *Rich Dad Poor Dad* has succeeded in lifting the veil of confusion, fear, and frustration around money and replacing it with clarity, truth, and hope for every person who is willing to commit to the process of coming financially educated.

In order to make good on the promise of financial literacy and ultimate freedom, Robert Kiyosaki assembled his own team of personal and trusted advisors, proven experts in their respective fields, to deliver the only complete 'how-to' series of books and programs that takes the messages of Rich Dad to the streets of the world and gives each reader the step-by-step processes to achieve wealth and income in business, investing, and entrepreneurship.

RDA Press is driven by several of Kiyosaki's actual Advisors who have committed to take the messages of Rich Dad, convert them to practical applications and make sure those processes are put in the hands of those who seek financial literacy and financial freedom around the world. The series gives practical, proven processes to succeed in the areas of finance, tax, entrepreneurship, investing, property, debt, sales, wealth management and both business and personal development. Three of these trusted and accomplished Advisors—Blair Singer, Garrett Sutton, and Ken McElroy—are the driving forces behind RDA Press.

RDA Press is proud to assume the role of publisher of the Rich Dad Advisor series and perpetuate a series of books that has sold millions of copies worldwide and, more importantly, supported tens of millions in their journey toward financial freedom.

The #1 Secret
That Helps Me Achieve
My Investing Goals:

Accelerate your learning and results by following Andy and his investing mentors every week.

They focus on generating profits no matter if the market is going up, or down, or sideways.

When you join Andy's Mentor Club, you'll have an insider's view of what he sees happening in the market, how he is adjusting his trades, and new trades of the week.

This is the ideal way to make the jump from learning about investing to actually making intelligent investments.

Join Andy's Mentor Club Today:
www.andysmentorclub.com

Notes